THE CAVE IN THE MOUNTAIN

A Sequel to *In the Pecos Country*

LIEUT. R. H. JAYNE

1st WORLD
LIBRARY
Literary Society

The Cave in the Mountain

Lieut. R. H. Jayne

© 1st World Library, 2007
PO Box 2211
Fairfield, IA 52556
www.1stworldlibrary.com
First Edition

LCCN: 2007930818

Softcover ISBN: 978-1-4218-4858-7
Hardcover ISBN: 978-1-4218-4761-0
eBook ISBN: 978-1-4218-4955-3

Purchase *"The Cave in the Mountain"*
as a traditional bound book at:
www.1stWorldLibrary.com/purchase.asp?ISBN=978-1-4218-4858-7

1st World Library is a literary, educational organization
dedicated to:

- Creating a free internet library of downloadable ebooks

- Hosting writing competitions and offering book publishing
scholarships.

Interested in more 1st World Library books? contact:
literacy@1stworldlibrary.com
Check us out at: www.1stworldlibrary.com

1ˢᵗ World Library Literary Society

Giving Back to the World

"If you want to work on the core problem, it's early school literacy."

- James Barksdale, former CEO of Netscape

"No skill is more crucial to the future of a child, or to a democratic and prosperous society, than literacy."

- Los Angeles Times

"Literacy... means far more than learning how to read and write... The aim is to transmit... knowledge and promote social participation."

- UNESCO

"Literacy is not a luxury, it is a right and a responsibility. If our world is to meet the challenges of the twenty-first century we must harness the energy and creativity of all our citizens."

- President Bill Clinton

"Parents should be encouraged to read to their children, and teachers should be equipped with all available techniques for teaching literacy, so the varying needs and capacities of individual kids can be taken into account."

- Hugh Mackay

CONTENTS

CHAPTER I

A STRANGE GUIDE

"Well, if he doesn't beat any one I ever heard of!"

Mickey O'Rooney and Fred Munson were stretched on the Apache blanket, carefully watching the eyes of the wild beast whenever they showed themselves, and had been talking in guarded tones. The Irishman had been silent for several minutes, when the lad asked him a question and received no answer. When the thing was repeated several times, he crawled over to his friend, and, as he expected, found him sound asleep.

This was not entirely involuntary upon the part of Mickey. He had shown himself, on more than one occasion, to be a faithful sentinel, when serious danger threatened; but he believed that there was nothing to be feared on the present occasion, and, as he was sorely in need of sleep, he concluded to indulge while the opportunity was given him.

"Sleep away, old fellow," said Fred. "You seem to want it so bad that I won't wake you up again."

The boy's curiosity having been thoroughly aroused, all tendency to slumber upon his part had departed, and he determined that if there was any way by which he could profit any by that wolf, he would do it.

"He may hang around here for a day or two," he mused, as he heard the faint tappings upon the sand, "thinking all the time that he'll get a chance to make a meal off of us. So he will, if we don't keep a bright look-out. It seems to me that he might be driven out."

The more he reflected upon this suggestion of his own, the more reasonable did it become. His plan was to drive out the wolf, to compel him to show up, as a card player might say. Considering the dread which all wild animals have of fire, the plan was simple, and would have occurred to anyone.

"The camp-fire seems to be all out, but there must be some embers under the ashes. Mickey threw down his torch somewhere near here."

Carefully raking off the ashes with a stick, he found plenty of coals beneath. These were brought together, and some of the twigs laid over, the heat causing them at once to burst into a crackling flame. This speedily radiated enough light for his purpose, which was simply to find one of those "fat" pieces of pine, which make the best kind of torches. A few minutes search brought forth the one he needed, and then, shoving his revolver down in his belt, he was ready.

The light revealed the large beautiful Apache blanket, stretched out upon the ground, while the Irishman lay half upon it and half upon the earth, sleeping as soundly as if in his bed at home. Beyond him and in every direction was the blackness of night. But, looking to his right, he discovered the two eyes staring at him and glowing like balls of fire.

The animal was evidently puzzled at the sight before him.

Lieut. R. H. Jayne

Fred dreaded a shot from the Indians above, and, as soon as he had his torch ready and had taken all his bearings, he drew the ashes over the spluttering flame. Save for the torch, all was again wrapped in impenetrable gloom.

The glowing orbs were still discernible, and, holding the smoking torch above his head, Fred began moving slowly toward them. The animal did not stir until the lad was within twenty feet, when the latter concluded that it would be a good thing for him, also, to take a rest.

"Wonder if he's been trained not to be afraid of torches," mused the little fellow. "I hope he hasn't, and I hope too there won't be any trouble in scaring him."

The lad dreaded another possibility,—that his torch might be suddenly extinguished. If that should go out, leaving them in utter darkness, the wolf would immediately rise to a superior plane, and speedily demonstrate who was master of the situation.

Fred swung the torch several times around his head, until it was fanned into a bright flame, after which he resumed his advance upon his foe. At the very first step the beast vanished. He had wheeled about and made off in a twinkling.

The lad pressed onward at the same deliberate gait, watching carefully for the reappearance of the guiding orbs. It was not long before they were observed a dozen yards or so further on. The wolf was manifestly retreating. He had no fancy for that terrible torch bearing down on him, and he was falling back by forced marches. This being precisely what Fred desired, he was greatly encouraged.

"He is making his way out, and after awhile he will reach the place, and away he'll go. If he's a wolf or fox, the hole may be so small that Mickey can't squeeze through, but I think I can follow one of the animals anywhere."

After going some distance further, Fred noticed that the animal was not proceeding in a straight line. He would appear on his right, where he would stare at the advancing torch until it was quite close, when he would scamper off to the left, and go through the same performance.

"He knows the route better than I do, so I won't try to disturb him," reflected the boy as he followed up his advantage, with high hopes of discovering the secret which was so important to himself and friend. "I won't crowd him too hard, either, for I may scare him off the track and fail."

The wolf was evidently a prey to curiosity—the same propensity which has caused the death of many bipeds and quadrupeds. The action of the torch puzzled him, no doubt. He had seen fire before, and probably had been burnt—so he knew enough to give it a wide berth; but it is doubtful whether he ever saw a flaring torch held over the head of a boy and solemnly bearing down upon him.

Fred's absorbing interest in the whole affair made him wholly unmindful of the distance he was traveling. He had already advanced several hundred yards, and had no idea that he was so far away from his slumbering friend. The fact was that the singular cave was only one among a thousand similar ones found among the wilds of the West and Southwest. Its breadth was not great, but the distance which it ran back into the mountains was amazing.

The wolf was leading the lad a long distance from the camp, and, what was more important (and which fact, unfortunately, Fred had failed to notice), the route was anything but a direct one. It could not have been more sinuous or winding.

Lieut. R. H. Jayne

The course of the cavern, in reality, was as winding as that of the ravine in which he had effected his escape from the Apaches, and from which it seemed he had irrevocably strayed. Had he attempted to make his return, he would have found it impossible to rejoin Mickey O'Rooney, unless the two should call and signal to each other.

However, the attention of the lad was taken up so entirely with the task he had laid hold of, and which seemed in such a fair way of accomplishment, that he took no note of his danger. The wolf was leading him forward as the *ignis fatuus* lures the wearied traveler through swamps and thickets to renewed disappointment.

"He has some way of reaching the outer world which the Indians haven't been able to find. Of course not; for, if they knew, they would have been in here long ago. They wouldn't stay fooling around that opening, where they're likely to get a shot from Mickey when they ain't expecting it. Now, if the wolf will only behave himself, all will come out all right."

Fearful of being caught with an extinguished torch, the lad kept up the practice of swinging it rapidly round his head every few minutes. When he ceased each performance, the flame was so bright that he was able to penetrate the darkness much further upon every hand.

On one or two of these occasions he caught a glimpse of the creature as it bounded away into the darkness. In shape and action it was so much like the mountain wolves which had besieged him some nights before that all doubts were removed. He knew it was one of those terrible animals beyond question.

"Wonder how it is he's alone? It wasn't long after I saw that old fellow the other night, when there was about fifty of them under the tree. One of them is enough for me, if he doesn't give us the slip. Maybe he has come in to find out how the land lies, and is going back to report to the rest."

Fred could not help reflecting every few minutes on the terrible situation in which he would be should his torch fail, and the other bring a pack of ravenous creatures about him. They would make exceedingly short work of a dozen like him.

"It seems good for hours yet," he said as he held it before him, and examined it for the twentieth time.

The stick was a piece of a limb about as thick as his arm, and fully a yard in length. It felt as heavy as *lignum vitae*, and, by looking at the end held in his hand and that which was burning, it could be seen that it was literally surcharged with resin—so much so that, after being cut, it had overflowed, and was sticky on the outside. No doubt this, with others, had been gathered for that express purpose, and there was no reason to doubt its capacity.

As Fred advanced he caught occasional glimpses of the jagged overhanging rocks, which in some places were wet, the water dripping down upon him as he passed. The fact, too, that more than once both sides of the cave were visible at the same time, told him that the dimensions of their prison were altogether different from what he had supposed.

"There must be an end of this somewhere," he muttered, beginning to suspect that he had gone quite a distance, "and I'm getting tired of this tramping. I hope the wolf hasn't gone beyond the door he came in by, and I hope he has nearly reached it, for it will take me some time before I can find my way back to Mick."

Lieut. R. H. Jayne

CHAPTER II

ALONE IN THE GLOOM

Before Fred could complete the sentence his foot struck an obstruction and he was precipitated headlong over and down a chasm which had escaped his notice. He fell with such violence that he was knocked senseless.

When he recovered he was in darkness, his torch having been extinguished. The smell of the burning resin recalled him to himself, and it required but a moment for him to remember the accident which had befallen him. For a time he scarcely dared to stir, fearing that he might pitch headlong over some precipice. He felt of his face and hands, but could detect nothing like blood. The boy had received quite a number of severe bruises, however, and when he ventured to stir there were sharp, stinging pains in his shoulders, neck and legs.

"Thank God I am alive!" was his fervent ejaculation, after he had taken his inventory. "But I don't know where I am or how I can get back again. I wonder what has become of the torch."

He could find nothing of his flambeau, although he was confident that it was near at hand. Fred believed that he had fallen about twenty feet, striking upon his chest and shoulders. At this juncture, he thought of the wolf which had drawn him into the mishap, and he turned his head so suddenly to look for him that the sharp pain in his neck caused him to cry out. But nothing of the beast was to be seen.

"Maybe he went over here ahead of me, and got killed," he thought; "but I don't think that can be, for a wolf is a good deal spryer than a boy can be, and he wouldn't have tumbled down as I did."

Fred recollected that he had several matches about him, and he carefully struck one upon the rock beside him. The tiny flame showed that he had stumbled into a rocky pit. It was a dozen feet in length, some three or four in width, and, when he stood erect, his head was level with the surface of the ground above. In consequence, it would be a very easy matter for him to climb out whenever he chose to do so; but above all things he was desirous of regaining his torch. Just as the match between his fingers burned out, he caught sight of it, lying a short distance away.

"It's queer what became of that wolf," he said to himself, as he recovered the precious fagot and painfully climbed up out of the pit. "Maybe he thought I was killed, and went off to tell the rest of his friends, so that they can all have a feast over me. I must fire up the torch as soon as I can, for I'm likely to need it."

This did not prove a very difficult matter, on account of the fatness of the torch, which ignited readily, and quickly spread into the same thick, smoking flame as before. But Fred noted that it was about half burned up, and he could not expect it to hold out many hours longer, as it had already done good service.

"I wish I could see the wolf again," he said to himself, looking longingly around in the darkness, "for I believe he entered the cave somewhere near here, and it was a great pity that I had the accident just at the moment I was about to learn all about it."

He moved carefully about the cave, and soon found that he had reached the furtherest limit. Less than twenty feet away it terminated, the jagged walls shutting down, and offering an impassable barrier to any further progress in that direction.

All that he could do, after completing his search, was to turn back in quest of his friend Mickey. The belief that he was in the immediate neighborhood of the outlet delayed the lad's return until he could assure himself that it was impossible to find that for which he was hunting, and which had been the means of his wandering so far away from camp.

Fred occupied fully an hour in the search. Here and there he observed scratches upon the surface of the rocks in some places. He was confident that they had been made by the feet of the wolves; but in spite of these encouraging signs, he was baffled in his main purpose, and how the visitor made his way in and out of the cave remained an impenetrable mystery.

"Too bad, too bad!" he muttered, with a great sigh. "I shall have to give it up, after all. I only wish Mickey was here to help me. I will call to him, so that he will be sure to hear."

As has been intimated in another place, the two friends had a code of signals understood by both. When they were separated by quite a distance, and one wished to draw the other to him, he had a way of placing two of his fingers against his tongue, and emitting a shrill screech which might well be taken for the scream of a locomotive whistle, so loud and piercing was its character.

When the lad uttered his signal, he was startled by the result. A hundred echoes were awakened within the cavern, and the uproar fairly deafened him. It seemed to him that ten thousand little imps were perched all around the cavern, with their fingers thrust in their mouths, waiting for him to start the tumult, when they joined in, with an effect that was overwhelming and overpowering.

"Good gracious!" he gasped, "I never heard anything like that. I thought all the rocks were going to tumble down upon my head, and I believe some must have been loosened."

He looked apprehensively at the dark, jagged points overhead. But they were as grim and motionless as they had been during the many long years that had rolled over them.

"Mickey must have heard that, if he is anywhere within twenty miles," he concluded.

But, if such was the case, he sent back no answering signal, as was his invariable custom, when that of his friend reached him. Fred listened long and attentively, but caught no reply.

"I guess I'll have to try it again," he added, with a mingled laugh and shudder. "I think these walls can stand a little more such serenading."

He threw his whole soul in the effort, and the screeching whistle that he sent out was frightful, followed, as it was, by the innumerable echoes. It seemed as if the walls took up the wave of sound as if it were a foot-ball and hurled it back and forth, from side to side, and up and down, in furious sport. The dread of losing his torch alone prevented the lad from throwing it down and clapping his hands to his ears, to shut out the horrid din. Some of the distant echoes, coming in after the others were exhausted, gave an odd, dropping character to the volleys of sound.

Had the expected reply of Mickey been the same as the call to him, the lad would have been deceived thereby, for the echoes, as will be understood, were precisely the same as answering whistles, uttered in the same manner. But Fred understood that, if the Irishman heard him, he would reply with a series of short signals, such as are heard on some railroads when danger is detected. But none such came, and he knew, therefore, that the ears which he intended to reach were not reached at all.

"I don't understand that," he mused, perplexedly, "unless he's asleep yet. When I left him, it didn't seem as though he'd wake up in a week. Perhaps he can hear me better if I shout."

A similar racket was produced when the boy strained his lungs, but his straining ear could detect no other result. It never once occurred to Fred that he and his friend were separated by such a distance that they could not communicate by sound or signal. And yet such was the case, he having traveled much further than he suspected.

Having been forced to the disheartening conclusion that it was impossible to find the outlet by which the wolf had escaped, Fred had but one course left. That was, to find his way back to the camp-fire in the shortest time and by the best means at his command. If the mountain would not go to Mohammed, then Mohammed would have to go to the mountain.

The lad began to feel that a great deal of responsibility was on his shoulders. The remembrance of Mickey O'Rooney going to sleep was alarming to him. He looked upon him as one regards a sentinel who sinks into slumber when upon duty. Knowing the cunning of the redskins, Fred feared that they would discover the fact, and descend into the cave in such numbers that escape would be out of the question.

And then again, suppose that their enemies did not disturb them, what was to be their fate? The venison in the possession of the Irishman could not last a great deal longer, and, when that was gone, no means of obtaining food would be left. What were the two prisoners then to do?

Mickey had hinted to Fred what his intention was, but the lad felt very little faith in its success. It appeared like throwing life away to make such a foolhardy attempt to reach the outside as diving into a stream of water from which there was no withdrawal, and the length of whose flow beneath the rock could only be conjectured, with all the chances against success. But Fred recalled in what a marked manner Providence had favored him in the past, and he could but feel a strong faith that He would still hold him in his remembrance. "I wouldn't have believed I could go through all that I have had in the last few days; and yet God remembered me, and I am sure He will not forget me so long as I try to do His will."

On the eve of starting he fancied he heard a slight rustling on his right, and he paused, hoping that the wolf would show himself again; but he could not discern anything, and concluded that it was the dropping of a stone or fragment of earth. The lad was further pleased to find, upon examination, that the revolver in his possession was uninjured by his fall. In short, the only one that had received any injuries was himself, and his were not of a serious character, being simply bruises, the effects of which would wear off in a short time.

"I hate to leave here without seeing that wolf," he said, as he stood hesitating, with his torch in hand. "He may be sneaking somewhere among these rocks, popping in and out whenever he has a chance; and if I could only get another sight of him, I would stick to him till he told me his secret."

He awaited awhile longer, but the hope was an illusive one, and he finally started on his return to camp.

CHAPTER III

STRANGE EXPERIENCES

Young Munson was destined to learn ultimately that he had undertaken an impossible task. The hunter, in the flush and excitement attending the pursuit of game, can form no correct idea of the distance passed, and so he, in attempting to run the shadowy wolf to earth, had traveled twice as far as he supposed. The case is altogether different when the hunter starts to return. It is then that the furlongs become miles, and the wearied pursuer feels disgusted with the enthusiasm which led him so far away from headquarters.

When the lad was certain that he had labored far enough on the back track to take him fully to the camp-fire, he really had not gone more than one-half the distance. Worse than this, he saw, from the nature of the ground, that he was "off soundings." Several times he was forced to leap over openings, or rents, similar to that into which he had stumbled, and the broadening out of the cave made it out of his power to confine his path to anything like reasonable limits. The appearance of unexpected obstructions directly in his way compelled numerous detours, with the inevitable result of disarranging the line he intended to pursue, and causing his course to be a zigzag one of the most marked character.

There were no landmarks to afford him the least guidance. In short, he was like the ill-fated steamer caught on a dangerous coast by an impenetrable fog, where no observations can be made, and the captain is compelled to "go it blind." He was forcibly reminded of this difficulty by unexpectedly finding himself face to face with the side of the cavern. When he thought that he was pursuing the right direction, here was evidence that he was at least going at right angles, and, to all intents and purposes, he might as well have been going in exactly the opposite course.

"Well, things are getting mixed," he exclaimed, more amused than frightened at this discovery. "I never tramped over such a place before, and if I ever get out of this, I'll never try it again."

But there was little cause for mirth, and when he had struggled an hour longer, something like despair began to creep into his heart. Worse than all, he became aware that his torch was nearly exhausted, and, under the most favorable circumstances, could not last more than an hour longer.

While toiling in this manner, he had continued to signal to Mickey in his usual manner, but with no other result than that of awakening the same deafening din of echoes. By this time he was utterly worn out. He had been traveling for hours, or, rather, working, for nearly every step was absolute labor, so precipitous was the ground and so frequent were his detours. He had accomplished nothing. When he expected to find himself in the immediate vicinity of the campfire, there were no signs of it, and the loudest shout he could make to his friend brought no reply.

This fact filled the mind of Fred with a hundred misgivings. He had given up the belief that it was possible for Mickey to remain asleep all this time. He was sure the night had passed, and, great as was the capacity of the Irishman in the way of slumber, he could not remain unconscious all the time. And then nothing seemed more probable than that he was placed for ever beyond the power of response. If a dozen Indians quietly let themselves down through the opening during the darkness of the night, they could easily discover the sleeping figure, and dispatch him before he could make any kind of resistance.

It was this fear of the Indians being in the cave that made the lad apprehensive every time he gave utterance to his signals. He believed they were as likely to reach the ears of the Apaches as those of Mickey, and his faith of the extraordinary shrewdness of those people was such that he did not doubt but that, by some means or other, they would learn the true signal with which to reply. As yet, however, no such attempt had been made, so far as his ears informed him, but his misgivings were none the less on that account. What was the use of their taking the trouble to answer when he was walking directly into their hands? There was a cowering, shrinking sensation from his own noise, caused by the expectation that a half-dozen crouching figures would leap up and swoop down upon him.

The darkness remained impenetrable, and, as Fred toiled forward, he was continually recalling the words of Byron, which he had read frequently when at school, and had learned to recite for his father. He found himself repeating them, and there was no doubt that he realized more vividly than do boys generally of his age the meaning of the author:

"The world was void:
The populous and powerful was a lump,
Seasonless, herbless, treeless, manless, lifeless;
A lump of death, a chaos of hard clay.
The rivers, lakes and ocean, all stood still,

And nothing stirr'd within their silent depths."

Such fancies as these were not calculated to make him feel particularly comfortable while carrying the torch. Such a person in such a situation makes an especially inviting target of himself, and, although Fred dreaded to see it burn itself out, when the chances were that he was likely to be in sore need of the same, yet he had wrought himself up to such a pitch that he more than once meditated extinguishing it altogether, with the purpose of putting himself on an equality with those of his enemies who might be prowling in the night around him.

"I wonder whether Mickey would be more likely to hear my pistol than a shout or whistle?" he said, as he drew the weapon from his belt and held it up to inspect it in the light of the flaring torch. "It seems to be all right, although there's no telling how long since it has been loaded. Here goes."

With this, he pointed the muzzle toward the cavern and pulled the trigger.

The response was as prompt as though he had charged the chamber but a short time before, proving not only that the weapon was of the best quality, but that the ammunition was equally so, and the slight moisture that characterized the atmosphere of the cave had not been sufficient to injure the charge. It seemed as if he had fired a cannon, the echoes rolling, doubling, and repeating on themselves in the most bewildering and terrifying fashion.

Fred could not understand how it was that such a pandemonium of sound could escape filling the subterranean world from one end to the other, and so he sat down on a ledge of rock to listen for some reply from his friend.

It was several seconds before the trickeries of nature, in the way of echoes, terminated and matters settled down to their natural quiet. And then, when quiet came again, it was like that of a tomb—deep, profound, and impressive. The bent and listening ear could detect nothing that could be supposed to resemble the noise of the cascade, which had excited his wonder when he was stretched out upon the ground directly above it.

"This must be about forty miles round," he said to himself, when he had waited for the reply until convinced that it was not forthcoming, "and I have strayed away altogether."

The luxury of rest was so great, after his long, wearying toil, that he concluded that he might as well spend a half hour in that fashion as in any other. The echoes and pains of his bruises had departed,—or, more properly, perhaps they were consolidated with the aches and pains following upon the overtaxing of his limbs.

"Oh, dear! How tired I am!" he sighed, as he stretched out his limbs. "It seems to me that I won't be able to walk again for a week. I must rest awhile."

His fatigue was so great that he was not conscious of any desire for food or rest.

"Maybe I will need that torch more after a time than I do now," he added, as he looked listlessly at it. "It seems good for a half hour yet, and I don't want it." With this he thrust the burning end in the sand at his feet, and held it there until it was entirely extinguished, and he was wrapped again in the same impenetrable darkness. So far as possible, he had become accustomed to this dreadful state of affairs. He had been viewing and breathing the atmospheric blackness for many hours, although it may be doubted whether one who had spent so much of his life in the sunshine could ever become accustomed to the total deprivation of it.

Fred had assumed an easy position, where he could lay his head back, and, straightening out his legs, he made up his mind to enjoy the rest which he needed so badly. When a lad is thoroughly and completely tired, it is difficult for him to think of anything else; and although, while walking, the fugitive was tormented by all manner of wild fancies and fears, yet when his efforts ceased, something like a reaction followed, and he sighed for rest, content to wait until he should be forced to face the difficulties again.

When he closed his eyes all sorts of lights danced before him, and strange, indescribable noises filled the air. It seemed that impish figures were frolicking all around, sometimes grinning in his face, and then skurrying far away through the aisles of the gloom. At last he slept. The slumber was sweet and dreamless, carrying him through the entire night, and affording him the very rest and refreshment which he so sorely needed.

This sleep was nearly completed when Fred was aroused by some animal licking his face. He arose with a start of exclamation and terror, and the animal growled and darted back several feet. A pair of gleaming eyes flashed in the darkness—the same pair which he had seen before. The wolf had come back to him.

Fred drew his revolver with the purpose of giving him a shot, when he reflected that it would be wisdom not to kill the animal until he was forced to do it in self defense. So he shoved the weapon back in its place, where it could be seized at a moment's warning, and sat still. In a few moments the wolf ventured softly up to him, and preparing to begin his feast. The boy, yielding to a strange whim, threw out his arms and made a grab at him.

The affrighted creature made a leap to escape the embrace, and Fred grasped his tail with both hands. This made the wolf wild with terror, and away he leaped. The boy hung on, running with might and main in his efforts to keep up. The brute, not knowing what he had in tow, was only intent upon getting away, and he plunged ahead as furiously as if a blazing torch was tied to his tail. Fred was fully imbued with the "spirit of the occasion," and resolved not to part company with his guide, unless the caudal appendage should detach itself from its owner. The wolf was naturally much more fleet of foot, but his efforts of speed only increased that of the lad, who, still clinging to his support, labored with might and main.

Away, away they went!

Now he was down on his knees; then clambering up again; then banging against the rocks—still onward, until he found himself flat on his face, still holding to his support, while the wolf was clutching and clawing to get away. They were in such a narrow passage way that Fred could not rise. Unclasping one hand, he held on with the other, while he worked along after him. For a long time this savage scratching, struggling and toiling continued, and then, all at once, Fred was dazzled by the overpowering flood of light.

He had escaped from the cave in the mountain, and was in the outside world again.

Lieut. R. H. Jayne

CHAPTER IV

SUNLIGHT AND HOPE

By clinging to the tail of the terrified wolf, Fred Munson had been assisted, dragged, and pulled from the Cimmerian gloom of the mountain cave into the glorious sunlight again. When the glare of light burst upon him, he let go of the queer aid to freedom, and the mystified animal skurried away with increased speed.

For a time the lad was so dazed and bewildered that he scarcely comprehended his good fortune. His eyes had been totally unaccustomed to light for so long a time that the retina was overpowered by the sudden flood of it and required time to accommodate itself to the new order of things. A few minutes were sufficient. And then, when he looked about and saw that he was indeed outside of the cave which had been such an appalling prison to him, Fred was fairly wild with joy.

It was all he could do to restrain himself from shouting, whooping and hurrahing at the top of his voice. It was only the recollection that there were a number of Apaches near at hand that sufficed to keep his voice toned down. But he danced and swung his arms, and threw himself here and there in a way that would have made a spectator certain that he was hilariously crazy. Not until he was thoroughly used up did he consent to pause and take a breathing spell. Then he gasped out, as well as he could, during his hurried breathing:

"Thank the good Lord! I knew He would not forget me. He let me hunt around for a while, long enough to make me feel I couldn't do anything, and then He stepped in. The wolf came. I didn't think I could make anything out of him, but I grabbed his tail. I held on and here I am. Thank the good Lord again."

When able to control himself still further, Fred made a survey of his surroundings. In the first place, he observed that the forenoon was only fairly under way, the sun having risen just high enough to be visible. The sky was clear of clouds and the day promised to be a beautiful one, without being oppressively warm.

"It is strange that I could not find the opening when the wolf scampered straight to it."

However, he did not stop to puzzle over the matter. It was sufficient to know and feel that he was back again in the busy, bustling world, saved from being buried in a living tomb.

An examination of the point where he had debouched from these Plutonian regions showed Fred that he was considerably below the general regions of the earth. He was in a sort of valley, surrounded by rocks and boulders, and the opening through which he had scrambled was situated sidewise, so that at a distance of ten feet it could not be seen. This accounted for the fact that none of the Indians knew any other means of ingress and egress excepting the opening in the roof of the cave. It was almost impossible to discover, except by accident or long continued and systematic search.

Fred's next thought was regarding Mickey O'Rooney, and he questioned himself as to the best means of reaching him, and assisting him to the same remarkably good fortune which had attended himself. The immediate suggestion, naturally, was to re-enter the cave and, after hunting up his old friend, conduct Mickey to the outer world, but it required only brief deliberation to convince him of the utter folly of such an attempt. In the first place, should he re-enter the cave, he would be lost again, not knowing in what direction to turn to find his friend and entirely unable to communicate with him by signal, as had been their custom when separated and looking for each other. Should he venture away from the tunnel to renew his search, it was scarcely possible that he could find his way back again. He would not only lose Mickey, but he would lose himself, with not the remotest chance of finding his way into the outer world again. So it was clearly apparent that, having been delivered from prison, it would not do for him to go back under any circumstances. He must remain where he was, and whatever assistance he could render his friend, must be given from the outside. How was this to be done?

To begin with, he felt the necessity of getting out of the circumscribing valley and of taking his bearings. He wished to learn where the opening through which he had fallen was situated. It was no difficult matter to work his way upward until he found himself up on a level with the main plateau. There, his view, although broken and interrupted in many directions, was quite extended in others, and his eye roamed over a large extent of that broken section of the country. He was utterly unable to recognize anything he saw, but he was confident that he was no great distance from the spot for which he was searching. It was only through the entrance that he could hold communication with Mickey, whenever the way should be left clear for him to do so. But he was fully mindful of the necessity for caution in every movement.

It was not to be supposed that the Apaches, having struck what might be called a gold-mine, intended to abandon it at the very time the richest of results were promised. And so, after long deliberation, the boy decided upon the direction in which the opening lay, and he made toward a small peak from which, in case his calculations were correct, he knew he would see it. Strange to say, his reckoning was correct in this instance; and when he stealthily made his way to the elevation and looked down over the slope, he saw the clump of bushes covering the "skylight," not more than a hundred yards distant.

He saw something else, which was not quite so pleasant. Six Apache warriors were guarding the same entrance.

"I wonder if they think Mickey expects to make a jump up through there!" was the thought which came to Fred, as he peered down upon the savages, and counted them over several times. "I don't see what they are to gain by waiting there, unless they mean to go down pretty soon."

He could not be too careful in the vicinity of such characters, and, stretching out flat upon his face, he peeped over the top, taking the precaution first to remove his cap, and then to permit no more of his head than was indispensable to appear above the surface. The six redskins were lounging in as many different lazy attitudes. One seemed sound asleep, with his face turned to the ground, and looking like a warrior that had fallen from some balloon, and, striking on his stomach, lay just as he was flattened out. Another was half-sitting and half-reclining, smoking a pipe with a very long stem. His face was directly toward Fred, who noticed that his eyes were cast downward, as though he were gazing into the bowl of his pipe, while Fred could plainly see the ugly lips, as they parted at intervals and emitted their pulls in a fashion as indolent as that of some wealthy Turk. A third was seated a little further off, examining his rifle, which he had probably injured in some way, and which occupied his attention to the exclusion of everything else.

The bushes surrounding the opening had been torn away, although it was difficult to conceive what the Indians expected to accomplish by such an act, as it only served to make them plainer targets to the Irishman, whenever he chose to crack away from below.

The remaining trio of Apaches were occupied in some way with the cavern. They were stretched out upon the ground, with their heads close to the orifice, down which they seemed to be peering, and doing something, the nature of which the lad could not even guess.

"That don't look as though they had caught Mickey," he muttered, with a feeling of inexpressible relief; "for, if they had, they wouldn't be loafing around there."

Nothing of their horses could be seen, although he knew they must have a number of them somewhere in the neighborhood. An Apache or Comanche without his mustang would be like a soldier in battle without weapons.

"I'd like to find them," thought Fred, lowering his head, and looking back of him. "I'd take one and start all the others away, and then there would be fun."

The lad had it in his power to take an important step toward his return to his friends. Nothing was more likely than that a little search through the immediate neighborhood would discover the mustangs of his enemies, which, as a matter of course, were unguarded, the owners anticipating no trouble from any such source. Mounted upon the fleetest of prairie rangers, it would not require long to reach the open country, when he could speed away homeward.

But to do this required the abandonment of his friend, Mickey O'Rooney, who would not have been within the cavern at that minute but for his efforts to rescue him from the same prison. It was hard to tell in what way the lad expected to benefit him by staying, and yet nothing would have persuaded him to do otherwise.

"I may get a chance to do something for him, and if I should be gone and never see him again, I should blame myself forever. So I'll wait here and watch."

The three redskins on the edge of the opening remained occupied with something, but the curiosity of the lad continued unsatisfied until one of them raised up and moved backward several steps. Then Fred saw that he had a lasso in his hand, and was drawing it up from the cave. He pulled it up with one hand, while he caught and looped it with the other, until he had nearly a score of the coils in his grasp. This could not have been the cord which held the blanket when the shot of Mickey O'Rooney cut it and let the bundle drop, for that was much smaller, while this was sufficient to bear a weight of several hundred pounds, it having been used to lasso the fleet-footed and powerful mustangs of the prairies.

"They've been fishing with it," concluded the youngster; "but I don't believe that Mickey would bite. What are they going to do now?"

After drawing up the rope, the whole half dozen Apaches

Lieut. R. H. Jayne

seemed to become very attentive. They gathered in a group and began discussing matters in their earnest fashion, gesticulating and grunting so loud that Fred distinctly heard them from where he lay. This discussion, however, speedily resulted in action.

Another of the blankets already described was very artistically doubled and folded into the resemblance of a man, and then the lasso was attached to it. The Apaches experimented with it for several minutes before putting it to the test, but at last everything was satisfactory, and it was launched. The aborigines seemed to comprehend what the trouble was with the other, and they avoided repeating the error.

When they began cautiously lowering the bundle, the six gathered as close to the margin as was prudent to await the result. Their interest was intense, for they had mapped out their programme, and much depended upon the result of this venture. But among the half dozen there was no one who was more nervously interested than Fred Munson, who felt that the fate of Mickey O'Rooney was trembling in the balance.

CHAPTER V

MINING AND COUNTERMINING

Fred expected every moment to catch the dull crack of the rifle from the subterranean regions as a signal that Mickey O'Rooney had neither closed his eyes to the impending peril, nor had given way to despair at the trying position in which he was placed. But the stillness remained unbroken, while the lasso was steadily paid out by the dusky hands of the swarthy warrior, whose motions were closely watched by the others.

Lower and lower it descended as the coils lying at his knees were steadily unwound, until the disturbed lad was certain the bottom of the cavern was nearly reached, and still all was silent as the tomb.

"I'm sure I would hear his gun if he fired it," he said, worried and distressed by what was taking place before his eyes; "and if I did not, I could tell by the way they acted whenever he pulled trigger. What can he be doing?"

The lad thought it possible that his friend was absent in some distant part of the cave hunting for him, and was, therefore, totally unaware of the flank movement that was under way. It could not be that he was still asleep; he had no fears on

Lieut. R. H. Jayne

that score. It might be, too, that the Irishman had arrived at the conclusion that the situation had grown so desperate as to warrant him in the *dernier resorte* he had fixed upon. If such was the case, then, as Mickey himself might have said, "the jig was up."

Two or three coils still remained upon the ground when the Apache stopped lowering the lasso, and, looking in the faces of his companions, said something.

"It has either reached the bottom of the cave, or else Mickey has fired at it," said Fred, who became more excited than ever.

He had caught no sound resembling a shot, and he concluded that it must be the former, as was really the case. In a few seconds the Indian began drawing up the lasso again, and a short time thereafter the roll of blanket was brought to the surface. It was carefully examined by all the group. The dirt on it proved that it had rested on the bottom of the cave, but there were no marks to show that it had received any attention at the hands of any one there.

There were grunts of pleasure, as this fact was gathered by the redskins. The experiments had been satisfactory and they were prepared to venture upon the more dangerous and decisive one—the one which they intended should bring matters to a focus.

Fred was in doubt what this plan was to be until he saw the blanket unfolded and as carefully wrapped around the form of one of the Apaches, encasing him from head to foot. Great pains were taken to hide his head and feet from view, the warrior lying upon his back, and suffering himself to be "done up" with as much thoroughness as if he were a choice sample of dry-goods. Viewed from a disinterested stand-point, the wonder was how he was to breathe in such wrappings.

"They have tried the blanket, and finding that was not disturbed, they're going to send down one of their number, thinking that if Mickey does see it he'll believe it is the same blanket, and won't fire at it, because he didn't fire at the other."

It looked very venturesome upon the part of the warrior thus to enter the lion's den. But while, as a rule, the Indians of the Southwest are treacherous and cowardly, there are occasional instances in which they show an intrepidity equal to that of the most daring white scouts.

When everything was arranged to the satisfaction of all, three of the most stalwart Apaches braced themselves, with the lasso grasped between them, while a fourth carefully piloted the body over the edge of the opening, and began slowly lowering it to the bottom.

The bravest man, placed in the position of the enwrapped redskin could not have avoided some tremor, when he knew that he was hanging in midair, in plain view of the rifleman who had separated the thong which supported the blanket in the first attempt. The Indian must have experienced strange emotions; but if he did, he gave no evidence. He remained as passive as a log, his purpose being to imitate the appearance of the first bundle.

"Now, if Mickey let's that go down without sending a bullet through it, he hasn't got one half the sense that I think he has."

Fred was hasty and impatient at the seeming success which marked everything that the red-skins undertook. He looked and listened for some evidence that the Irishman was "there;" but no dull, subterranean report told him of the fatal rifle-shot, while the three Apaches continued steadily lowering their comrade with as much coolness and deliberation as if not the slightest particle of danger threatened. Minute after minute passed, and the lad was in deep despair. It could not be, he was compelled to think, that Mickey O'Rooney was anywhere in the vicinity. He must be a long distance away, searching for his young friend, not knowing, and, perhaps, not caring about the Apaches. He might consider that, within the darkness of the cave, they all had an equal advantage, and he could hold his own against each and every one. There was no denying that the defender had a vast advantage over those who might come into his "castle," provided he was really aware of their movements, but it was this doubt that caused the boy his uneasiness.

"He must be near the bottom," he concluded, when this paying-out process had continued some minutes longer, and he thought he saw very little of the lasso left.

Such was the fact. Only a few seconds more passed, when there was a general loosening up on the part of the redskins, as in the case of men who have just finished a laborious job. They looked into each others faces, and there were guttural exclamations, as if they were congratulating themselves upon what had been accomplished.

"And, now, what next?" asked the disgusted watcher. "Good luck seems to go with everything they undertake, and I suppose they'll bring Mickey up by the heels."

But such was not the sequel, and probably not the expectation of the Apaches. They had succeeded in planting a man in the breach, and their purpose was to follow him, as they speedily proved. The behavior of the group around the opening showed that the Indians were holding communication with their ally below, probably by a system of signals with the lasso, such as the man in the diving-bell employs when below the surface. These, too, must have been satisfactory, for, in a very brief time thereafter, the decisive operations were taken up and continued.

There was considerable of the lasso still left above ground—more than Fred imagined—and this was secured about a jutting point in a rock near at hand. It was fixed so immovably that it could not fail. "I wonder if they mean to roll that thing in upon Mickey's head, or what is it?"

They speedily showed what their intentions were. In less than a minute after the lasso was fastened, one of the Apaches caught hold of it and slid down through the opening so rapidly, that it looked as if he had lost his hold and dropped out of sight. A second did precisely the same thing; then a third, fourth and fifth, until only one warrior was left above ground.

"Oh! I hope he'll go," whispered Fred to himself; "and then I can do something big."

But the Apaches had evidently concluded that it would be an imprudent arrangement not to leave any of their friends on guard—not because they expected any interference from outside parties, but to provide against accident. If the lasso should fail them at a critical moment, they would be in a bad predicament, cut off from all means of getting out, as the skylight was the only avenue known to them, while, if a comrade remained above, all such danger would be escaped. Their purpose had been to send the five warriors down into the cave to attend to the case of the parties there.

The redskins were now down below and the whole thing was

put in shape for operations to begin. All that remained was to find their man, and Fred could not tell what the prospects of success were in that direction; but he was almost ready to believe that they were all that the Indians could ask. The sixth Apache, who remained visible, took matters very comfortably. He stretched himself flat upon the ground, with his head hanging almost in the opening, so that he could catch every sound that came up from below. It was plain that he expected to be called upon to render important service, and he did not intend to let a signal escape him.

The hour that succeeded made little change in the situation. The action of this redskin showed that he occasionally received and sent messages—most probably by the subterranean telegraph—but he shifted his position very little. While he was thus engaged, Fred Munson was intently occupied with another scheme, and he had speedily wrought himself into a high pitch of excitement.

"I believe I can do it," he muttered, more than once, as he revolved the desperate scheme in his mind; but, whatever his plan was, he waited in the hope that fortune would appear more propitious.

When the Apache had sat thus for some time, he changed his position. He had been lying with his side toward the lad, but now he sat up, with his back to him, and as close to the edge of the opening as was prudent, while he held the lasso in his hand, like the fisherman on the bank of a stream, who patiently waits and is sensitive to the slightest nibbling at the other end of his line.

He had scarcely settled himself in this position when Fred Munson changed his own. Rising from the ground where he had lain so long, he stepped over the ridge, and advanced directly toward the redskin, who harbored no suspicion that there was any of his race in his neighborhood. The plan the lad had resolved upon required nerve, resolution and quickness. He stepped as lightly as was consistent with speed until he had passed half the distance, when he began to slacken his gait and to proceed with greater caution than ever.

All depended upon his ability to keep from being heard or detected. Of course, he had no wish to engage in a fight with one of these fierce warriors, but he was prepared, even for that. His hand rested upon the hilt of his revolver, so that he could whip it out at an instant's warning and discharge it, as he meant to do if necessary.

It was while he was yet some distance from the redskin that Fred felt that his position was one of frightful peril. His foe had his rifle within easy reach, and, if he turned too soon, he could pick off his young assailant before he should arrive within striking distance,—but each moment raised the hopes of the lad.

Lieut. R. H. Jayne

CHAPTER VI

A DARING EXPLOIT

A veteran Comanche warrior could not have advanced with greater skill than did young Munson approach the unconscious Apache. The warriors who had taken this little business in hand seemed to have cleared away the treacherous ground surrounding the opening, so that it was not likely to give way beneath their weight, even when they advanced close to the edge. The single redskin who remained seemed to have shifted his position more for the purpose of relieving himself from his cramped posture than anything else.

He was standing erect, about a foot away from the edge, with the lasso in both hands, looking down into the cavern of gloom below, listening and watching, with the sense of touch also on the alert. His blanket and rifle lay at one side, out of the way, but where they could be reached at a single leap, if necessary. The end of the lasso was still fastened to the rock, but the savage held it loosely, so that the slightest twitch upon it would become known to him on the instant.

It is not often that an Indian can be taken off the guard. Years of danger have made the senses of the savages preternaturally acute, and they are as distant as the timid antelope of the plains. But, for all that, there was a boy within a dozen yards of a swarthy warrior whose senses were on the alert, and yet had failed to detect his proximity.

Fred gazed upon him with the fixed intensity of the jungle tiger stealing upon his prey. With his right hand resting upon the hilt of his revolver, he never removed his eyes from the muscular figure of the Apache, bending over the entrance to the cavern.

"Shall I shoot, or push him over?"

This was the question the lad kept revolving in his mind, as he advanced step by step. With the pistol he could bury two or three balls in the body of the redskin before he could suspect where they came from, and thus completely clear the path before him. But there were doubts in the way. The revolver might miss fire, in which case all hope would be gone. In a hand-to-hand tussle the Apache would be more than a match for a dozen such lads. True, the weapon had not failed when he pulled the trigger in the cave, but there was no certainty that it would not do so when he most needed it.

Then, too, he felt a natural repugnance against stealing upon a foe in this fashion, and shooting him in the back. It had a cowardly look, even when certain that the threatened party would have done precisely the same thing, had the opportunity come in his way.

"I will push him over, if he don't make me shoot him."

But to do this necessitated a much closer approach. He must literally be within "striking distance." Could he place himself there without discovery? If the redskin were asleep, or if his mind was occupied with something of a different nature, or if there were some extraneous noise, the case would be different. The blowing of the wind, the murmur of a waterfall (such as Fred had heard when lying upon the ground in the same spot) would have been a most fortunate diversion. But there was nothing of the kind. There was a dead calm, not a breath of air stirring, and the day was hot.

Fred had approached within twenty feet, and still the Apache did not stir. How vivid and indelibly his appearance was impressed upon the vision of the boy! He could never forget it. The redskin, although of powerful build, was anything but pleasing in appearance, even when viewed from the rear.

His blanket being thrown aside, he was naked, with the exception of a breech-cloth. His feet were of large size, encased in shabby moccasins, while frowsy leggins dangled between the knee and ankle. His body, from the breech-cloth to the shoulders, was splashed and daubed with a half dozen kinds of paint, while his black, thin hair straggled about his shoulders and was smeared in the same fashion. Like most of the Indians of the Southwest, he wore no scalp-lock, but allowed his hair to hang like a woman's, not even permitting it to be gathered with a band, nor ornamenting it with the customary stained eagle-feathers. His arms were also bare, with the exception of the wrists, around which were tied bracelets, which, no doubt, he considered very attractive. The boy could fancy what a repulsive face he possessed.

Step by step, inch by inch, the young hero made his way, his eyes fixed upon the savage with a burning intensity, until it seemed that he would burn him through and through. And the Apache heard him not, although they were no more than ten feet apart.

"He will hear the thumping of my heart," was the constant fear of the boy.

Slowly lifting one foot, he put in on the ground as softly as if it were held in a slipper of eiderdown. He was treading upon a thin growth of grass, interspersed plentifully with gravel, but he never once looked to see what he was stepping upon. Indeed, he could not remove his eyes from the one central figure of his thoughts and vision.

One obstruction, no matter how slight—the turning of a pebble, a slip, even the most trivial, and the Apache would turn like lightning, and be upon him in a flash. Two more steps were taken, and only eight feet separated the lad and the Indian, and still the latter remained all unconscious of what was going on. Fred's heart was throbbing violently, but he retained control of himself. He felt that the critical moment was close at hand. A slight advance more, and the attempt was to be made.

He grasped the handle of the revolver more firmly than ever, but he raised his foot for another step, feeling that the distance was still too great. At this juncture the Indian moved!

He stepped one pace backward directly toward the boy, and he looked up and away. But not behind him. The glance was a mere casual one. He had heard nothing, and he expected to see nothing, when he looked off in the manner mentioned.

The Apache remained standing in this attitude for a minute. Then he stepped forward and resumed his former position on the edge of the opening, still clinging to the lasso, as if in constant expectation of some signal.

During this little episode Fred remained as motionless as if cast in bronze. His eyes were still centred upon the Indian, and he partially drew his revolver from the girdle he wore about his body, with the expectation of using it. But when his foe gave his attention to the cave below, the lad softly

Lieut. R. H. Jayne

shoved the weapon back in its place, and again raised his foot.

The movement was slow and painful, but it was accomplished successfully. Only a single step more remained to place him where he wanted to be. That taken, and one bound was all that he needed to make. Finally, and for the last time during the advance, the right foot ascended from the ground, was poised for a few seconds in the air, and then came down with the same care as before. But it touched a loose pebble which turned with the lightest imaginable noise.

As quick as a flash the Apache raised his head, looked in front, and then darted his vision from left to right, when his keen eyes detected something crouching behind him.

At the very instant of the discovery, Fred concentrated all his energies in one effort, and bounded forward like a catapult. The distance was precisely what it should have been, and, as he threw out his hands, he struck the Indian squarely in the back with the whole momentum of the body. In fact, the daring boy nearly overdid the matter. He not only came near driving the Apache to the other side of the opening, but he came equally near plunging himself down it. As it was, the victim, taken completely off his guard, was thrown against the other side, where his wonderful dexterity enabled him to throw out his hands and check his downward descent.

Fred, after his narrow escape from going down into the cave, scrambled back to his place, and saw the Indian struggling upon the opposite side, with a good prospect of saving himself. "That won't do," was his thought, as he ran round the opening so as to bring himself directly before him. "I don't want you up here."

Thrusting his pistol almost against his painted forehead, he fairly shouted:

"Get down—let go, or I'll shoot!"

Whether the Apache possessed much knowledge of the English tongue can only be conjectured, but the gestures accompanying the command were so expressive that he could not fail to take in the whole meaning. The Indian, no doubt, considered it preferable to drop down into the pit rather than run against the bullet. At any rate, he released his hold, and down he went.

As he drooped into the gloom he made a clutch at the lasso, doubtless for the purpose of creeping up unawares upon the lad, who, by a strange providence, had so suddenly become his master. But the Indian, although a pretty good athlete, had not practiced that sort of thing, and he failed altogether, going down to join his comrades much the same as if he had dropped from a balloon.

Fred proved himself equal to the emergency. The moment he saw that he was relieved from the presence of his enemy, he darted back to the other side of the opening, caught hold of the lasso, and hurriedly drew it up out of reach of those below.

"There! they can't come crawling up that when I ain't thinking," he said, when the end of the thong was in his hand.

He coiled the whole thing up at his feet, and then, with a feeling of relief and pleasure which cannot be described, he looked about to see whether he was alone. Alone he was, and master of the situation. Where there had been six daring Apache warriors a half-hour before, not one was now visible. All were in the cave. Five had gone willingly, while it looked very much as if the sixth had not been so willing. At any rate, they were all beyond the power of injuring Fred Munson, who, after considering over the matter, concluded that he had done a pretty good thing.

CHAPTER VII

FISHING FOR A FRIEND

"I think I dumped that Apache down there just as nicely as any one could have done it," said Fred, as he sat upon the ground. "It must have taken him by surprise when I banged into his back that way. I'd like to know whether he fell on his head or feet. He hadn't much time to get ready for the fall, and so maybe it wasn't just as he wanted it. I don't think it was, either, with Mickey or me. Such things ain't generally in this part of the world. Maybe some of the others were standing around, and this fellow went down on their heads. If he did, it must have shaken all their dinners up. That's a pretty good way to fall down there, and although I didn't get hurt much, I wouldn't want to try it again."

Fred had had remarkable success, but there was a question as to what he was going to do with it. He was on the outside of the cavern, with the means at command for assisting Mickey to the surface, but, the Indians being down below, it was not clear how this was to be done, as they were likely to take a hand in the matter.

As preliminary to any elaborate attempts in that direction, it was necessary that he should apprise him of his presence, and establish some sort of communication with him. This,

Lieut. R. H. Jayne

under the circumstances, was exceedingly difficult, as it was not likely that the Irishman would suspect that his young friend had succeeded in reaching the outside until he had received strong proof of it. Very fortunately, however, the couple possessed a code of signals which were easily understood, if they were only heard.

"I will try him on our old call," said Fred, as he crept as close to the edge as he deemed safe, and emitted a whistle that must have extended far within the cave.

"If he hears that, he will understand it," he added, turning his ear, so that he could catch any response; but the dim, soothing murmur of the cascade was the only sound that came up from the cavernous depths.

"He must be there—he must be there, and he will come back, so he will catch the signal sooner or later."

There was one aspect of the business which had not yet occurred to Fred, and which was likely to inure to the benefit of Mickey O'Rooney, the gentleman who just then stood in need of everything that came along in that line. The Apaches were skillful and wise enough to learn from the trail which had first told them the story, that a boy and man had been caught in the cavern, and it was very evident that they all believed that there was no other avenue of escape except that by which they had entered. At the same time, their knowledge of the peculiarities of their own country must have convinced them that it was possible that other openings, of which they knew nothing, might exist, and might become known to the prisoners.

The last Indian who went down must have known that the lad who assisted him was one of the parties for whom they were yearning, and his presence was proof that he had made the fortunate discovery which was denied the natives of the territory. If the lad had emerged by that means into the outer world, the natural supposition would be that his companion had done the same, and that, therefore, neither of the fugitives were below, the inevitable conclusion being that the tables had been completely turned upon them. Such was certain to be the conclusion of the Apaches, and it remained for Mickey O'Rooney to use ordinary prudence and keep himself out of the way of the redskins, to secure a chance of further outwitting them by a bold piece of generalship.

Fred repeated his whistle four or five times, with an interval of ten minutes, when his hopes were raised to the highest pitch by hearing it answered. In his excitement he thrust his head far over the opening, gave the signal again to prevent mistakes, and listened.

A full minute elapsed, when the reply came, sounding faint and far away. It showed that Mickey was at a considerable distance from the opening, and that he heard and understood the situation. To make matters still more certain, the lad now shouted at the top of his voice, holding both hands so as to inclose his mouth like a tunnel.

"Mickey, I'm up here with a lasso! Nobody else is here! Whenever you can get the chance, get hold of the lasso, and climb up! I will let it down after a while!"

It cannot be said that this was a very wise proceeding upon the part of the lad; for it was likely that some one of the half dozen Apaches understood English well enough to comprehend what he said. To clinch the business, Fred yelled a few more words.

"If you understand me, Mickey, whistle!"

The words were no more than fairly uttered when the desired response was made, faintly, but, nevertheless, distinctly.

"That's good," concluded the delighted lad. "Now all I have to do is to wait for him to get the chance, and he will come up the lasso, and then we'll be done with the cave."

This, certainly, was all that he had to do, but, at the same time, this amounted to a good deal.

"Now, if I let this rope down," added the lad, as he thought the matter over, "one of those Apaches will try to climb up it, and I will have to cut it, and that will leave it in his hands, and then what will become of Mickey?"

He debated a long time as to the best plan of overcoming this serious difficulty; but none presented itself, and he concluded that it was an inevitable contingency, which he must prepare himself to defeat, at all hazards.

Fred had been so absorbed with the business which had succeeded admirably up to this hour, that he scarcely noted the passage of time. He was not a little amazed when he came to look at the sun and to note, from its position, that the afternoon was considerably advanced, and that night was much nearer than he supposed. Nearly twenty-four hours had elapsed since he had tasted food, and, although he felt somewhat faint, he was not troubled with hunger. He made up his mind to make no effort to obtain food until he should succeed in bringing the Irishman from his prison—as he hoped to do before the night should pass away. But he was thirsty, and, believing that he could quench his thirst without going very far, and without jeopardizing the safety of his friend, he started off on a little hunt for water.

"That stream runs out of the cave not very far from here, and, if I can find that, it will be just what I want."

Fixing in his mind the direction of the stream, he started off, taking an almost opposite direction from that which led to the ridge, where he had lain so long watching the movements of the Apaches. This led him directly behind a mass of boulders and rocks, tossed irregularly together, and surrounded by a peculiar growth of stunted vegetation, with rich, succulent grass beyond.

Fred was hurrying along, with no thought of seeing anything unusual, when he was startled by coming directly upon a half dozen mustangs, all bound to the limbs or trunks of trees with strong lariats, while they were lazily cropping the grass where they had been left undisturbed for several hours. They were all fine-looking animals, every one of them—not one having saddle or bridle, and nothing, indeed, excepting the long thong, which, like the lasso, was made of bull's hide, and which prevented them from straying beyond their appointed limits. There could be no doubt that the animals belonged to the little party taking an airing in the cave, and the eyes of the lad sparkled as they rested upon them.

"Oh! if Mickey were only here!" he exclaimed to himself; "we couldn't want anything nicer. We would just pick out two of the best here, stampede the others, and then gallop toward home as fast as we could, and we'd be there inside of two or three days; but I must wait, and so must he."

The place selected by the Indians for their horses could not have been better chosen. In addition to the rich pasture, a rivulet of clear, cold water flowed by, within reach of each and all, so that all their wants were supplied in the best manner possible.

Every one of the mustangs raised their heads and looked up

at the stranger, and one or two gave a faint whinney, as if to inquire the business of such a character with them.

"I don't believe any of you can go like my Hurricane that I had to leave at home; but I can't have him, and I would be mighty glad to take one of you—that is, if Mickey could go along, for I don't intend to leave him, so long as I know he's alive. You seem pretty well fixed, so I'll let you alone till we get a chance to turn you to account, and you can eat and get yourself in good condition."

He took a good long draught of the refreshing water, and then made a little survey of his surroundings.

"I should like to know whether those six Indians were all looking for *me*. Maybe Lone Wolf has found out that I gave the three the slip, and he sent a half-dozen fresh ones to look me up. They were all strangers to me, and I am sure I never saw them before. Lone Wolf seems to want me very bad, and if these don't bring me back pretty soon, he may send somebody after them."

A careful survey of all the suspicious points failed to show him anything alarming, and he made his way back to the mouth of the cavern, where he sat down to await the moment for him to lower the lasso that he hoped was to give Mickey O'Rooney a chance for his life. It seemed to him that it would not be safe to attempt it until the sun went down. His theory was that the Apaches would not remain directly beneath the opening all the time, but that there would be a chance for the Irishman to creep up without detection. He would be looking for the lasso, and in the darkness might be able to ascend it without discovery.

The lad hoped that all the redskins had reached the conclusion that both he and the man were outside; and, finding that it was out of the question for them to escape by the opening, which was at such a distance over their heads, had scattered to search for some other egress. It was not impossible that such was the case, and if it were, it placed the situation in a light by no means discouraging.

It was hardly dark when Fred Munson carefully shoved the end of the rope over the edge of the opening, and let it descend slowly, gently and noiselessly to the bottom, permitting it to pass through his hands in such a way that he could tell the instant it was disturbed. When he knew that it had struck, he waited for a "bite."

To his astonishment, it came within the next five minutes. He was startled by feeling a decided pull repeated several times.

The situation was so delicately critical that it would not do to speak nor whisper, nor even to utter their whistle, no matter how cautiously made. So, by way of reply, Fred gave the lasso, several responsive jerks, intended to signify that everything was ready, and his friend might come ahead.

A moment later the lariat was jerked from his hand, showing that a heavy weight had suddenly fastened upon it, and the man was making his way upward from the cave.

Lieut. R. H. Jayne

CHAPTER VIII

FISHING FOR A PRIZE

It is no easy task, even for a trained athlete, to climb forty or fifty feet of rope. The majority of men, if put to the test of making their way out of that cave by shinning up the long lariat suspended from the opening above, would have failed altogether.

Remembering how well his hearing had served him under somewhat similar circumstances, young Munson, watching so anxiously for the appearance of his friend, pressed his ear against the tough, untanned rope and listened. He could hear the scraping of the hands and the friction of the limbs against the rope, working steadily and in such a manner as to show that the man was succeeding well in the excelsior business and was sure to reach the top in time, if his strength held out.

"I guess that's Mickey O'Rooney climbing up," muttered the boy, "and yet I can't tell till I get a sight of him. It may be an Apache, and I'd better get ready, for I don't mean to have any of them creeping up on me."

Fred did not wish to cut the rope, as that would have ended the operations, so he concluded to resort to his weapon. There were two or three chambers of the revolver undischarged and he did not believe that it would be necessary to use them. The simple presentation of the muzzle had accomplished his purpose some hours before, and there was little doubt that it would do the same thing again.

The sky was absolutely free from clouds, and the moon, near her full, shed such a light over the scene that the lad almost dreaded the result.

While all remained profoundly dark in the cave, at the moment the man reached the surface and was brought into relief against the sky beyond, he would be distinctly visible to any one who might be looking upward, and half a dozen rifles pointed and fired at that juncture could scarcely fail of fatal results. The lad's misgivings increased as the man neared the top. When he again applied his ear to the lariat, he could understand that the fellow was working hard, and could only be a few feet below him.

"There's nothing like being ready," he concluded, as he straightened up, and, rising to his feet, stood, pistol in hand, ready for the issue.

He stepped back several feet, where his vision was entirely unobstructed.

"If it's an Indian, he won't have a chance of showing anything more than his head, and if he don't take that out of the way in a hurry, I'll let a ray of moonlight through it."

He stood thus, as rigid as a statue, fully appreciating the difficulties of his position and the fatal consequences of allowing himself to be outwitted.

"Mickey, is that you?" he asked, in a cautions whisper, a moment later.

Lieut. R. H. Jayne

As he asked the question he noticed that work upon the rope instantly ceased.

"It's Mickey," he said to himself, "but he doesn't think it safe to speak."

Then to him: "All right old boy, come ahead, and you may do the speaking after you land. Come ahead—you're near the top."

Again the toiling climber resumed his labor, and he was within a foot or two of the opening. One more hitch and he would emerge into the moonlight.

"Come old fellow, give me your hand," he added; "you've had pretty hard work."

Just then the bronzed face of an Apache Indian, smeared with paint and contorted with eager passion, slowly rose in the moonlight. The exhausted warrior, feeling that the critical moment was at hand, when all depended upon prompt and decisive work, made furious efforts to clamber out of the cavern before the lad who held the key of the situation could prevent.

Although Fred had contemplated this issue, and had prepared for it, yet he had become so thoroughly imbued with the belief that it was Mickey O'Rooney who was toiling upward that he was almost entirely thrown off his guard. Because of this, the cunning Apache would have secured his foothold and clambered out upon the daring lad, but for one thing. He had done, tremendous work in climbing a rope for such a distance, and his strength was nearly gone when he reached the open air.

Before he could reap the reward of all this labor, Fred

recovered. Whipping out his revolver as before, he shoved it directly into his face, and said: "You ain't wanted here, and you'd better leave mighty quick!"

The warrior made a clutch at the weapon so close to him, but his exhaustion caused a miscalculation, and he failed altogether. He was supporting himself at this moment by one hand, and he acted as if the single effort to secure the pistol was to decide the whole thing. He failed in that, and gave up.

Instead of letting go and going to the bottom in one plunge, he began sliding downward, his head vanishing from sight almost as suddenly as if the lasso had been cut. It is generally easier to go down than up hill, and the work of twenty minutes was undone in a twinkling. A rattling *descendo*, and the Apache was down the rope again, standing at the bottom of the cave, and Fred was again master of the situation.

"Goodness!" exclaimed the lad, when he realized this gratifying state of affairs, "I had no idea that that was an Indian; but I ought to have suspected it when I called to him and he didn't make any answer. That stops that little sort of thing; but I don't know when Mickey is going to get a chance at the rope."

The lad was disheartened by this great disappointment, for it looked very much as if the redskins would guard all approaches to the lower end of the lasso, and his friend be shut out from all participation in the chance that he was so confident was placed at his disposal.

"I don't know what they can do with the rope," thought the lad, as he carefully took it in hand, "but then it's no use to them, and I may as well keep it out of their reach while I can."

He gently pulled it, to test whether it was free.

No one at that juncture seemed to have hold of it, and, fearful that it would not remain so, the lad gave it a sudden jerk, which brought it far beyond the reach of any one who might be gathered on the sand below.

"That upsets all my calculations," said Fred, with a sigh. "The chance of getting out of here is poorer than ever. I am afraid Mickey is in a scrape where there ain't much show of his helping himself!"

The lad remembered, however, that his friend still had one resort—the last one—at his command. When it became absolutely apparent that no other way was open, he would make the plunge down the stream, and risk all in the single effort to dive from the inside to the outside of the cave.

"I don't want him to try that, just yet," added Fred, as he lay upon the ground, carefully considering the matter; "for I think that will wind up the whole thing."

The boy seemed to be considering every phase of the question, and he debated with himself for a long time whether he couldn't do something for his friend. He thought of going back to the entrance by which he had escaped— thanks to the assistance of the wolf—reenter it, without going to a distance which would cause any danger of losing his way, and signal to him. The great obstacle to this was that, as he could readily see from the distance he had gone over since emerging therefrom, it would be utterly impossible to send a signal so far, through such a chamber of sound as the cave had proven itself to be. There remained the same probability that the Apaches would hear it as soon as Mickey, and they would be stupid beyond their kind if they had not already gained a correct idea of the situation.

Still, it was possible to see how the Irishman could succeed. Men placed in fully as desperate situations as he had pulled through by showing nerve and readiness of resource when the critical moment should arrive.

Mickey O'Rooney possessed originality and pluck. He had acquired considerable experience and knowledge of Indian "devilments" on his way across the plains, and, if the Apaches comprehended the situation, it was not to be supposed that he was not posted fully as well. If he could see no chance of getting a pull at the rope, he could easily keep out of the way of the redskins. He had no fear of meeting any of them singly, and if he could arrange it so as to encounter them one after another, and at his own convenience, he might clear the track in that fashion.

As it was, therefore, Fred Munson could only await for the issue of events. He was powerless to do anything until the sign should be made by his friend at the other end of the rope.

For fully two hours things remained in *statu quo*. The lad lay upon the ground close to the opening, listening, looking and thinking so intently that there was no danger of his falling asleep. The profound stillness remained unbroken during all that time. The murmur of the cascade had a faint, distant sound, as if it came from the ocean, many long leagues away, but there was nothing more—not even a signal from Mickey, who, if he had any plans, was working them with admirable secrecy. At the end of that time the lad concluded that it would be best to lower the lasso again.

"If he is down there, he must have a chance to get hold of the rope, or he can't come up here," was the reasonable conclusion of the lad, who passed it downward slowly and in perfect silence.

Fully a score of theories flitted through his head as he lay thus speculating upon the situation down below. At one time he was sure that it was useless to attempt to help his friend in that style. A half-dozen Apaches would not permit a single white to climb into safety immediately before their eyes, especially when they could cover him with their rifles if he should succeed in giving them the slip at the start. Then it appeared anything but reasonable to suppose that the Indians would remain directly below him, waiting for their chance to try their fortune in the trapeze line again. More likely they would scatter and hunt separately for the outlet which had permitted their intended victim to gain his safety. They could expect to gain nothing by remaining, and they were too shrewd to do so.

When the matter presented itself in this shape, Fred was ready to call down to Mickey, instructing him to grasp the lasso, and ascend without further delay. Too much precious time was being wasted. Fortunately, however, before he acted upon this theory, enough doubts arose to prevent his carrying it out.

He had had enough experience with the rope to know how to gauge it very well, and he lowered it until the other end was within two or three feet of the bottom. Having placed it thus within easy reach, he let it pass over his hand, holding it so delicately poised that the slightest disturbance was sure to be detected. He was in the position of the fisherman who is angling for some plump piscatorial prize, which requires the most skillful kind of persuasion to induce him to nibble the hook.

For a half-hour nothing touched it, and then Fred fancied that he felt a slight jerk. He made no response, but instantly became all attention and waited. A second later the jerk was repeated so distinctly that there could be no mistake. The lad gave it a twitch in reply, and then all remained still for a short time. Suddenly the thong was snapped from his hand, and instantly became taut.

Fred applied his ear as before. Yes; some one was climbing up the rope again.

CHAPTER IX

GROPING IN DARKNESS

It is proper, at this point, to introduce some history of the movements of Mickey O'Rooney, after the separation between himself and his young friend. The latter, it will be remembered, left him sleeping upon the Apache blanket, at the bottom of the cave, while he, the lad, went off in pursuit of the wolf, which came so near leading him to destruction, but which, in the end, conducted him to freedom and safety.

The Irishman slept for several hours longer, as soundly as if he lay in his own bed at home. He was sorely in need of sleep, and, having convinced himself that there was no danger to be apprehended, he transferred all his anxiety over to his young friend while he sailed off into the land of dreams. When he awoke and recalled where he was, he spoke to Fred; but, receiving no reply, supposed he was asleep, and passed his hand about in quest of him. After groping several minutes in vacancy, he muttered:

"Be the powers! if he hasn't fell out of bed, as me brother Tom used to remark to the ould gintleman, after he'd kicked me out of the same. The fall ain't far enough to hurt him seriously, but these laddies have a way of getting hurt, where a man couldn't do it, if he tried."

After calling and searching further, he struck a match and held it up. A transient glimpse was gained of an area of several hundred feet, in which, it is needless to say, he saw nothing of his young friend.

"Be the powers! but he strayed away," added Mickey, somewhat impatiently. "He thought there was something that it would pay to chase, and he's gone off, and, of course, will be lost."

With a view to bringing him back, the Irishman called his name, whistled, and, after a time, fired his gun. The echoes were not so loud as when Fred had fired, but the racket was sufficient to make him confident it would reach the ears of the boy, if he were not asleep or injured.

Mickey, as will be seen, formed the right opinion of the action of his young friend, and hoped that he would be able to work his way back to camp, as they called it, without any mishap or assistance from him.

"He thinks there's another door that opens into the sunshine, and that isn't locked, and, if it is, he can pick the kay. He may work away till he becomes weary, and then he'll be back here, and we'll hare to contrive some other way, or it may be that good luck will lead him to the opening for which he sighs. Heaven grant that the same may be the case."

He waited, and watched, and hoped, as the hours passed by, until he began to believe that something serious had happened to him. At intervals he repeated his signals, but on no occasion was there anything like a response.

It was an odd juxtaposition of events that, at the very moment he uttered some of the calls, the despairing kid was doing the same thing, and, although each strained his ears to the utmost, yet neither suspected the truth.

The hours and the time passed on, until happening to look up at the opening, Mickey saw the prepared blanket slowly descending, just as Fred looked upon it from the ridge.

"I'm obliged to yees," he said, in an undertone, "but I don't find myself in pressing naad of the same. I have one here, but if ye insist on my taking that, I'll not quarrel with yees."

He resolved that when it came down within his reach he would cut the lasso, and take it, but before it reached the ground he had changed his mind.

He knew what the intention of the Apaches was, but he was not deceived for an instant.

"I'll not do anything at all," he muttered; "I'll not interfere, where it's so difficult to decide upon me duty, as the owld lady observed when the bear got her husband down. I'll let 'em think I'm aslaap, and see what they'll do."

And thus, as the reader already knows, the rolled-up blanket was lowered and raised again without molestation, almost grazing the upturned face of the Irishman as it did so.

"And the next will be one of the spalpeens himself. Begorrah! there he is this minute!"

Just as he anticipated, a short time after the blanket began its descent, enfolding the form of one of the swarthy warriors, the Irishman at once detecting the ruse.

His rifle was brought to his shoulder, but yielding to a whim, which he could hardly explain, he lowered it, without firing, resolved that he would do nothing at all, unless compelled to in self-defense. About this time an idea began to dawn upon him that silence and inaction upon his part might do himself more good than the most vigorous defense.

He might shoot the first Indian, and then the others would only keep themselves out of reach, and he would be no nearer escape than before. On the other hand, if he studiously forced himself into the background, they might begin to believe that he had discovered the means of exit which was unknown to them. He had no fear of not being able to keep out of their way, where he had such abundant room and where no light possibly could reach the interior and reveal his presence to a hundred searchers. If they chose to attempt to carry torches, then he could pick them off at his own convenience.

And so it came about that Mickey stood quietly by, and permitted the whole five Apaches to slide down the rope like so many monkeys, while he raised no hand in the way of protest. Not knowing how many the party numbered, he could not conjecture how many were left when the five had come down, and the business stopped for the time, but he knew, as a matter of course, that they would not enter the cave without leaving reinforcements upon the surface.

By the time the last man landed, Mickey had moved back to a point a hundred yards away from where the group were gathered, where he was seated upon a large rock.

"If any of 'em undertakes to flash a bull's eye in me face, I kin dodge down behind the same," was the way in which the Irishman reasoned it.

At such a time, and in such a place, the faculty of hearing was about the only one that could be counted upon, and, sliding softly off the rock, Mickey applied his ear to the earth. If the Apaches were moving about, the noise made by their feet was so slight that he could not be certain whether they were actually branching out and groping for him, or whether they were the sounds produced by the natural shifting of the feet of a group of men standing together.

Matters stood thus for some time, when the last Indian suddenly came through the opening and plumped down upon the ground below, his start on this journey being such that he was probably considerably shaken up by the involuntary trip.

"Ye spalpeens must be more careful in coming down-stairs," muttered Mickey, who supposed that the whole thing was an accident, as in his own case.

But it was not long before he heard the voice of Fred Munson, calling from above, and, as each word was distinctly heard, there was no room for any misunderstanding of the situation. The Irishman was literally dumfounded.

"Be the powers! if it isn't the most wonderful thing that ever happened, as Mrs. Murphy remarked when Tim came home sober one night. That laddy, in hunting around, has struck upon some hole that leads out, and he's forgot, or else it was so hard to find his way back to me, he has gone round to that place, and now hollers down at me.

"Begorrah," added Mickey, a moment later, "it must be that he shoved that spalpeen overboard, and there isn't anybody left up there in the way of Apaches but one, and he ain't an Apache, but a gintleman named Fred Moonson. Here's to his health, and if this thing gets any more delightful, I'll have to give a whoop and yell, and strike up the Tipperary jig."

The exultant fellow had hard work to keep his spirits under control when he fairly understood the brilliant exploit that had been performed by his young friend.

"It is almost aqual to my gineral coorse," he he added; "but I must try and hold in till I can get the laddy by himself. Then I'll hammer him, out of pure love, as ye may say."

Mickey managed to contain himself, but did not attempt to reply to the direct call which was made upon him. That, in one sense, would have been fatal, as it would have "uncovered" his position. The Irishman was quick-witted, and it occurred to him that the last incident which had happened at the entrance to the cave might be turned to good account. If he continued to remain in the background, the Apaches were likely to conclude that he, too, was beyond their reach.

Thus matters stood until the signal was made to him, when he deemed it wise to make a cautious reply, merely to apprise the lad that he was there within call, and understood the situation through and through.

Mickey was very apprehensive when, some time after, he discovered that one of the Indians was ascending the rope. He was not so apprehensive when he came down again. The result of this repulse was much more decisive than Fred had supposed. The warriors seemed to suspect that they were throwing away time in attempting to outwit one who held such an immense advantage over them, and who was too wide-awake to permit them to steal a march upon him.

The delighted Irishman knew, from the sounds, that the redskins were moving away from the spot, not with the idea of staying away altogether, but that they might engage upon a little reconnoissance which might possibly open the way that they were so anxiously seeking. One of the redskins passed almost within arm's length of him, never suspecting, as a matter of course, that he was brought into such proximity to a mortal enemy. Mickey only breathed until assured that there was quite a distance between him and the Apaches.

"Now it begins to look as though there's a chance for me," he concluded; "and if me laddy will let down the lasso, I'll thry the bootiful experiment of shinning up it, though I much fear me that it will be the same as a greased pole."

He moved with the utmost circumspection toward the spot, being able to locate it by means of the moonlit opening overhead, and when he was near it he halted and listened.

"I don't obsarve that any one is loafing about here, getting in the way of honest folks."

Just then he ran plump against an Apache, whom he did not suspect was so near him.

The redskin uttered a grunt of anger, no doubt suspecting that it was one of his own friends.

As quick as lightning the Irishman drew back and struck a blow that stretched the warrior senseless.

"I'll tache ye to be grunting around here when a gintleman runs again ye. Ye ought to be ashamed of yourself."

Mickey had already strapped his rifle to his back, and, groping about, he felt the end of the lasso dangling in front of his face. The same instant he grasped it and began the ascent.

CHAPTER X

"HERE WE ARE AGAIN!"

Fred Munson, having been deceived once by the Apache climbing up the rope, was not to be caught again in the same way. When he became certain that a second person was coming up, he grasped his pistol again, and held himself in readiness to "repel boarders," the very instant they appeared.

It soon became evident that this second person, whoever he was, had a serious time in climbing up the rope. He frequently paused as if resting, and this fact led the lad to feel more hopeful than ever that it was his old friend drawing near.

When it became apparent that he was near the top, the curiosity of Fred became so great that he drew himself forward, and, peering down the black throat of the cave, asked, in a whisper:

"I say, Mickey, is that you? Speak, if it is, or give a little whistle."

"Be the powers, but I'm so tired I'm spaachless, wid not even the strength to let out a whistle."

This established the identity of the climber beyond all question, and the words were hardly uttered when the familiar face of the Irishman appeared.

He was exceedingly tired, and the lad reached his hand down to assist him out. It was at this juncture that the Apache, who had run against the fist of Mickey O'Rooney, recovered, and seeing his foe in the act of vanishing, gave a whoop of alarm to his companions, caught up his rifle and fired away. The hasty aim alone prevented a fatal result, the bullet clipping the clothing of the Irishman.

"Fire away, ye spalpeens, for all the good it may do ye," called out the Irishman, who at this moment clambered out of range and sank down upon the ground.

"Begorrah, I'm as tired as Jim O'Shaughnessey after his friendly match with his wife," gasped Mickey, speaking shortly and rapidly, as best he could, while he leaned over upon his elbow, until he could regain his strength and wind.

It required but a short time, when he reached his hand to the lad, and shook it for the third or fourth time, smiling at the same time in his old jolly way, as he rose rather unsteadily upon his pins.

"I'll have to wait a while till the kink gets out of me legs, before I give ye the Donnybrook jig, but I make the engagement wid ye, and the thing is down for performance, do ye mind that? And now, me laddy, we must thravel. Are ye hungry?"

"Yes."

"I have a bite saved that'll do ye till the morrow. When ye waltzed out the cave and left me to meself, I felt there was no knowing how long I'd have to stay behind, so I knocked off both eating and drinking, with the idea of getting used to going without anything."

As they were able to talk more understandingly, the two explained their experiences since they had parted. They could not fail to be interesting in both cases. When they had finished, Mickey O'Rooney had about recovered from the terrible strain he had undergone in clambering out the cave, barring a little ache in his arms and legs.

"Now, me laddy, we must emigrate, as there ain't anything to be gained by loafing round here, as the gals used to tell the chaps when they tried to cut me out. The first thing to larn is whether the hoss that I lift some distance away is still there cropping the grass. If he is, then we shall have small work in making our way back to New Boston; but if he has emigrated ahead of us thar, we must hunt for others."

"There's no need of going that far."

"Why not?"

"Because the mustangs of the Apaches are right over yonder behind those rocks."

"That's good; let's take a look at the same."

They hurried over to the spot where the half dozen mustangs were tethered. They were lying upon the ground, taking their sleep, having finished a bounteous meal. The intelligent creatures showed their training by throwing up their heads the instant the two came in sight, and several gave utterance to whinneys, no doubt with the purpose of apprising their masters of the approach of strangers. None of them rose to their feet, however, and Mickey and Fred moved about, inspecting them as best they could in the moonlight, with the purpose of selecting the best.

"They're all a fine lot, as the neighbors used to say, after inspicting me father's family, and it's hard to make up your mind which is the best, but here is one that shtrikes me fancy. Get up wid ye."

The steed, spoken to in this peremptory manner, leaped to his feet, and stood in all his graceful and beautiful proportions, an equine gem, which could not fail to command admiration.

"I think he'll suit," said the Irishman, after a careful examination. "I think he can run as well as any of 'em. I'll tell you what we'll do, me laddy. We'll both mount this one, and ride till we reach the place where I lift mine, when we'll have one apiece."

"But if yours isn't there?"

"Then we'll kaap this one betwaan us, as the gals used to say, when they quarreled over me."

"Hadn't I better take one of the horses, and if we find yours, why, we can turn one of these loose, and we shall be all right, no matter how the things turn out?"

"It's not a bad idaa," assented the Irishman. "Pick yours out, and then we'll turn the others loose."

"Why will you do that?"

"What's the use of laving them here? Them spalpeens will find their way out of the cave before long, and then they will strike straight for these animals, and, if they happen to get out pretty soon, they'll make trouble with us. We might as well let 'em walk awhile."

"How are they going to get out?"

"Didn't ye lave the lasso hanging down into the cave?"

"I declare, I never thought of that!" exclaimed the affrighted lad. "Why didn't you tell me?"

And he started to repair the oversight, when Mickey caught his arm and checked him.

"Not so, me son; lave it as it is. If we should go away and lave the spalpeens down there without the rope, they might never find the way out, and would starve to death, and it would always grieve me to think I had starved six Apaches to death, instead of affording meself some enjoyment by cracking 'em over the head wid a shillelah."

"I should be sorry to do that," replied Fred, who comprehended the cruelty of leaving the poor fellows to perish, as they were likely to do if left without the means of escape; "but, if we leave the rope hanging there, the whole party will be up here before we can get out of the way, and then what shall we do?"

"Niver fear, niver fear," said Mickey, with a wave of his hand and a magisterial shake of the head. "The spalpeens have got enough of climbing up there for a while. They've gone off on a hunt through the cavern for the place where you crawled out, and they'll kaap at that till morning, and then, if there's no show for 'em, they'll come back, and begin to fool around the rope again."

The lad had little difficulty in deciding upon his steed, which was a coal-black mustang, lithe and willowy, and apparently of a good disposition, although that was necessarily a matter of conjecture, for the present. There were no saddles upon any of the horses, and nothing but the rudest kind of bridle, consisting of a thong of twisted bull's hide, and reaching away to some limb or tree, so as to give the animal plenty of grazing area. The lariats of the other four were cut—so that, when they arose, they would find themselves at liberty to go whither they chose—after which the two approached their respective prizes and prepared to mount.

Both were good riders, although, being compelled to go it bareback, they felt some misgivings as to the result. Fred's mustang was rather under size, so that he was able to vault upon him from the ground without difficulty. After patting him on the neck and speaking soothingly to him, with a view to disarming him of all timidity, the lad leaped lightly upon his back.

The steed showed at once that he did not like this familiarity, and reared and plunged and shook his head in a vicious way, but he toned down somewhat after a time, and seemed disposed to compromise matters until he learned something about his rider.

"Ye're going to become a good rider—that is, in the course of twenty or thirty years," remarked Mickey, who had been watching his young friend closely, "if ye practice aich day in those thirty years; but I want you to observe *my* shtyle—note how complately I bring the animal under, how docile he becomes, how mild, how gentle, how lamblike."

And with these rather pompous observations, he laid his hand upon the mane of his mustang, and at one bound bestrode him, catching the lariat after the manner of one who was determined to have no nonsense about it.

"Now note how quick I'll subdue him, how afeard he'll be, you can't goad him into trying to throw me. Talk about Rarey breaking that old horse Cruiser, that used to ate his keeper every day for breakfast, he couldn't compare wid mesilf."

Before Mickey had time to finish his observation, the heels of the mustang went up almost perpendicularly in the air, and with such suddenness that Mickey was thrown a dozen feet over his head, alighting upon his hands and knees.

Fred was amused beyond expression at the discomfiture of his boasting friend, who was not a little astonished at the manner in which he had been overthrown.

"Turns up," he said, as he gathered himself on his feet again, "that I was a little mistook. Such accidents will happen now and then, and it isn't very kind for a spalpeen like yourself to laugh at me sorrow."

"I can't help it, Mickey, but I'm afraid I can't stick to the back of this horse. He seems scared and mad, and his back feels mighty slippery without any saddle or blanket."

"Maybe, if I get on wid ye, the weight of us both will hold him down."

The mustang which hard thrown the Irishman continued to flourish his heels and disport himself in such a lively style, that his spirit became contagious, and the four, who were yet upon the ground, now came to their feet, and after some plunging and rearing, made a rush down the slope, and were soon out of sight.

The animal ridden by the lad showed a disposition to join them, but the rider resisted, and managed to hold him, until at the opportune moment, Mickey placed himself on his back, and, as he was really a good horseman, and used vigorous means, he speedily managed to bring him under control. Turning his head toward the ridge, they started him forward, pausing near the mouth of the cavern long enough to gather up one of the blankets lying there, as it was likely to be useful at no distant time.

CHAPTER XI

THROUGH THE MOUNTAINS

The moon was high in the sky, and it was near midnight. O'Rooney, who had taken upon himself the task of guiding the mustang, continued him on up the ridge, directly toward the spot where Fred had lain so long watching the action of the Apaches gathered around the opening of the cave.

The mustang walked along quite obediently, seeming to feel the load no more than if it was only one half as great. But those animals are like their native masters—cunning and treacherous, ready to take advantage of their riders whenever it happens to come in their way.

"Which is the raison I cautions ye to be riddy for a fall," said Mickey, after referring to some of the peculiarities of these steeds of the Southwest. "The minute he gits it into his head that we ain't paying attention, he'll rear up on his fore-feet, and walk along that way for half a mile. Not having any saddle, we'll have to slide over his neck, unless I can brace me feet agin his ears, and ride along standing straight up."

The constant expectation of being flung over the head of a horse is not the most comforting sensation that one can have, and the lad clung fast to his friend in front, determined not to

Lieut. R. H. Jayne

go, unless in his company. Upon reaching the top of the ridge, the horse was reined up for a few minutes, as Mickey, like the mariner at sea, was desirous of taking an observation, so as to prevent himself going astray.

"Can you remember how you were placed?" asked the lad, after he had spent several minutes in the survey; "that is, do you know which way to go for the horse you left eating grass?"

"I was a little puzzled at first, as me father obsarved to the school-teacher when he said I had been a good boy, but I see how it is now. It must have been that I got a little turned round when I was down in the basemint of these mountains, but I see how it is now. Right yonder," he added, pointing toward the Northwest, "is where I left my hoss, and there is where I hope I'll find him again."

"Is the road so that we can ride the mustang all the way there, or must we walk?"

"I remember I come right along some kind of a path, made by animals, after leaving the beast. I s'pose it's the route taken by the crathurs in going to the water, for there's a splendid spring right there, and the path that I was just tilling you 'bout leads straight to it."

"Then keep the horse from throwing us off, and we're all right. After we find your horse, Mickey, or don't find him, what are we to do, then?"

"Set sail for New Boston."

"But we can't ride through these mountains, if we don't find the pass."

"And the same is what we're going to do, barring that it hasn't been lost yet."

"Are you sure you know the way to it from where you left your horse? I've been hunting for it for hours, but couldn't any more tell where it was than the man in the moon. What course would you have to take to reach it?"

"Right off yonder," replied Mickey, pointing to the left.

"And I was sure that it was here," said Fred, pointing his hand in nearly an opposite direction.

"Which the same is a good raison why you're wrong. When you git lost, and think you're on the right way, ye may be sure that ye're wrong; and after figuring the whole thing over, and getting sartin of the right coorse, all you've got to do is not to take it, and ye're sartin of saving yerself."

"Then, according to that, you ought not to take the route which you have said is the right one."

"I'm spaking for lost spalpeens like yoursilf," said Mickey, severely. "I haven't been lost since I parted company with Soot Simpson, and, begorrah, that minds me that we ought to saa something of him. Just look around and obsarve whether he is standing anywhere beckoning to us."

Both used their eyes to the extent of their ability, but were unable to discover anything that bore a suspicious resemblance to a man.

So far as they could judge, they were entirely alone in this vast solitude.

"Do you expect to meet Sut very soon?"'

"Av coorse I do; why shouldn't I?"

"But he went another way from you altogether after Lone Wolf."

"That's just it. He wint another way, and wint wrong, and he has been gone long 'nough to find out the same."

"When he will turn back and follow you?"

"As soon as he finds he's wrong, he'll go right, and as I wint right, he'll be on my heels."

"But you know both of us have strayed a good deal off the track, and we have traveled in many places, where we haven't made the slightest trail. How is he going to follow us then?"

The Irishman gave utterance to a scornful exclamation.

"I've been with that Soot Simpson long enough to learn something. I've saan some specimens of what he kin do. Rocks don't make no difference to him. When he gits on the track of a wild bird, if it don't take extra pains to dodge and double, he'll foller its trail through the air. Oh, he's there all the time, and the wonder with me is that he hasn't turned up before."

"What would he have done had he come along and found us both in the cave, and the Apaches watching?"

"He would have tracked that wolf back to his hole, come in and fetched us out, and then slipped up behind the six, and tumbled them all in like so many tenpins."

"If he's such a wonderful man as that, it's a pity we couldn't have kept him with us all the time, and if we do run against him, we can afford to stop thinking about Apaches, as they will be of no account."

"Yees are right; but the trouble is to find him, as the man said when the British Government condemned John Mitchel, and him thousands of miles away in Ameriky. This thramping about at night in the mountains isn't the aisiest way to diskiver a man, and it's him that will have to find us, instead of we him. But we'll keep it up."

If the Apache mustang which they were riding meditated any mischief, he seemed to be of the opinion that the occasion was not the most suitable. He walked along with great docility and care, picking his way with a skill that was wonderful. Several times they approached places where it seemed impossible for an equine to go forward, but the horse scarcely hesitated, toiling onward like an Alpine chamois, until, at last, they drew up in a small valley, through the middle of which ran a small stream, that sparkled brightly in the moonlight.

"Here we are," said Mickey. "here's the spot where I left my cratur a couple of days ago, and where I don't see him just now. Use your eyes a bit, and tell me whether you obsarve him."

Fred was scarcely less anxious than his friend to recover the steed, for, recalling his experience in that line, he had good reason to mistrust Indian horses. It would be very awkward, when they should find a party of Apaches howling and rushing down upon them, to have the animal turn calmly about and trot back to his former friends, carrying his two riders into captivity, or leaving them to shift for themselves.

Nothing could be seen of the creature, but there was a fringe

Lieut. R. H. Jayne

of wood on the opposite side where he might be concealed, and Mickey slid off the blanket with the intention of hunting for him.

"Don't let this spalpeen give ye the slip," he cautioned the lad, as he gave the lariat into his hand; "for if mine is gone, this is the only one we have to depend on, and we can't spare him."

Fred felt a little uncomfortable when he found himself alone and astride of the fiery steed, which pricked up his ears as though he meditated mischief; but the horse seemed to think better of it, and continued so quiet that the young rider ventured to transfer his attention from him to Mickey, who was moving across the open space in the direction of the wood upon the opposite side.

The moonlight was so clear that he could be as plainly seen, almost, as if it were midday. As he moved along, he brought his rifle around to the front, so that he could use it at a moment's need, for he could not but see the probability that, if his horse had been lately disturbed, it was likely that those who did so were still in the vicinity, and no place was more likely to be used for a covert than the same patch of timber which he was approaching.

"Be the powers! but it looks a little pokerish!" he said to himself, slowing his gait, and surveying the wood with no little distrust. "There might be a dozen of the spalpeens slaaping there wid one eye open, or all sitting up and expicting me."

He had proceeded so far however, that it was as dangerous to turn back as it was to go on, for if any enemies were there, they were so close at hand that they could easily capture or shoot him before he could reach his horse. He was scarcely moving, and doing his utmost to penetrate the deep shadow, when, beyond all question, he heard a movement among the trees. He paused as if he had been shot and cocked his rifle, looking toward the point from whence came the noise.

"Aisy there, now," he said in a solemn voice. "I won't stand any of your thricks. I'm savage, and when I'm that way I'm dangerous, so if yees are there spake out, or else come out like a man, and tell me your name, be the token of which mine is Mickey O'Rooney from Ireland."

This characteristic summons produced no response, and, feeling the peculiar peril of his exposed position, the Irishman determined upon changing it and securing the shelter of a tree for himself. It was not prudent to move directly toward the spot which gave forth the rustling sound, as that would be likely to draw out a shot from a foe if he desired to avoid a personal encounter. Accordingly, the Irishman made what might be termed a flank movement by turning to the right, running rapidly several paces and then diving in among the trees, as though he were plunging into the water for a bath.

The few minutes occupied in making this change were those which Mickey felt were of great danger; for, if he should reach the wood and find himself opposed to but a single man, or even two, the situation would not be so uneven by any means. No shots were fired, and he drew a great sigh of relief when he gained the desired covert.

"Now I can dodge back and forth, and work me way up to them," he concluded; "and when they stick their heads out from behind the trees, I'll whack 'em for 'em, just as we used to do at Donnybrook when the fun began."

He waited where he was for some time, in the expectation

Lieut. R. H. Jayne

that his foe would reveal himself by an attempt to draw out. But if there is any one thing which distinguishes a scout, whether white or red, at such a time, it is his patience. It is like that of the Esquimaux, who will sit for sixteen hours, without stirring, beside an airhole in the ice, waiting for a seal to appear. Mickey O'Rooney was not burdened with overmuch patience, and acted upon the principle of Mohammed going to the mountain. He began picking his way through the shadows and among the trees, determined to keep forward until the mystery was solved.

CHAPTER XII

THROUGH THE MOUNTAINS
CONTINUED

When Mickey found himself under the shelter of the trees, something like his old confidence returned.

"As I obsarved some minutes ago, it's mesilf that's not going to stand any fooling," he added, loud enough for the redskins to hear. "Whither ye're there or not, ye ought to spake, and come out and smoke the calomel of peace, and give a spalpeen a chance to crack your head, as though ye're his brother; but if ye're up to any of your thricks, make ready to go to your hunting-grounds."

By this time he was within a dozen feet of the spot whence came the rustling that so disturbed him, and was staring with all his eyes in quest of the redskins. In spite of the bright moonlight, the Irishman could not be certain of anything he saw. There were trees of large size, behind any of which an Indian might have shielded himself effectually, and it was useless for Mickey to look unless his man chose to show himself.

The Irishman had all the natural recklessness of his race, but he had been in the Apache country long enough to learn to tone it down, for that was the country where the most fatal attribute a man could have was recklessness or rashness. In many instances of conflict with Indians it is worse than cowardice.

But, in the face of Mickey's assurance to the contrary, he did not feel altogether easy about the Apaches he had left at the cave. His humanity had prevented him from depriving them of means of escape, and although he was inclined to believe that they were not likely to climb the lasso until many hours should elapse, there could be no certainty about it. They might do so within an hour after the departure of the man and boy.

It was this reflection that caused Mickey to act with something of his natural rashness. He felt that he could not afford to wait to fight the thing out on scientific principles, so he determined, since he was so close, to force it to an issue without delay. Accordingly, he prepared himself to charge.

"I've been too kind already in giving ye warnings," he added, gathering himself for the effort, "and if your indifference causes your ruin, it's your own fault, as the bull remarked when he come down on a butt agin the engine."

Compressing his lips, Mickey made his start, forcing out a few words, as he would shoot bullets on the way.

"Nobody but a spalpeen of a coward would keep out of sight when he saw a head coming down on him in such tempting style as mine. I can't understand how he could."

In his furious hunt for antagonists, the belligerent fellow did not think of looking upon the ground. He made the blunder of Captain John Smith, of the Jamestown Colony, who, in retreating from Powhatan's warriors, became mired, with the eventual result of making Pocahontas famous, and securing an infinite number of namesakes of the captain himself.

Mickey O'Rooney had scarcely begun his charge when his feet came into violent collision with a body upon the ground, and he turned a complete somersault over it.

"Be the powers! but that's a dirty thrick!" he exclaimed, gathering himself up as hurriedly as possible, and recovering very speedily from his natural bewilderment. "A man who drops in the ring without a blow is always ruled out, and be that token ye're not entitled to the respect of illegant gintlemen."

During the utterance of these words the Irishman had carefully returned, boiling over with indignation and fight, and at this juncture he discovered the obstruction which had brought him to grief.

So far as appearances went, there was no Indian nearer than the cave. It was his own horse that had made the noise which first alarmed him. While the equine was stretched upon the ground, peacefully sleeping, his bumptious owner, in charging over his body, had stumbled and fallen.

Mickey was thrown "all in a heap" for a minute or two, when he found how the case stood, and then he laughed to himself as he fully appreciated the situation.

"Well, well, well, I feel as chape as Jerry McConnell when he hugged and kissed a gal for two hours, one evening, and found it was his wife, and she felt chaaper yet, for she thought all the time that it was Mickey O'Shaughnessy. I suppose me old swateheart," he added, as he stooped down and patted the head of his horse, "that ye've been living so high here for two or three days that ye're too fat to be good for anything. Come, up wid ye, ye old spalpeen!"

The mustang recognized the voice of his master, and obeyed as promptly as a child, coming upon his feet with the nimbleness of a racer, and ready to do what he was bidden. Mickey led him out into the moonlight, when he left him standing, while he went a short distance for the saddle and bridle, which he had concealed at the time of leaving the spot. They were found just as he had left them, and he returned in high feather, secured them in a twinkling upon his animal and galloped back to where the lad was waiting.

"Ye haven't seen or heard anything of redskins, have ye, while I was procuring my cratur?"

"Nothing at all," replied the lad; "but I heard you talking pretty loud, so I suppose you must have found several."

"No," answered Mickey, who did not care about explaining the whole affair. "I'm always in the habit of exchanging a few words wid the cratur when I maats, and such was the case a short time since, when I met him, after being away so long."

"Well, Mickey, we haven't any time to spare."

"Ye're right, my laddy; all you've got to do is to folly me."

With this he headed his mustang at precisely right angles to the course they followed in making their way to the spot; and Fred, who expected all sorts of trouble in the way of traveling, noticed that he was following some sort of path or trail, along which his horse trod as easily as upon the open prairie. While this was an advantage in one respect it had its disadvantage in another. The presence of a trail in that part of the world implied that it was one made and traveled by Indians, who were likely to be encountered at any moment, and Mickey was not insensible to the peril. But, in the present instance, there seemed to be no other means of getting along, and thus, in one sense, they were forced into it. The probabilities, however, were that they would soon emerge into safer territory, where it would be possible to take some precautions against pursuers.

For some time the two galloped along without speaking. The hoofs of their mustangs rang upon the rocks, and rattled over the gravel, and, in the still night, could have been heard a long distance away. While the Irishman kept as good a lookout ahead as possible, Fred Munson did his best to guard their rear. He kept continually glancing over his shoulder in the expectation of seeing some of their enemies, but nothing of the kind occurred, and before he anticipated it, they emerged into what seemed a deep valley, with high rocks upon both sides. Mickey drew up, and allowed his young friend to move alongside.

"Do ye mind ever having seen this place before?" he asked.

"I don't remember anything about this country, and all I ask is that we may get out of it as soon as possible."

"But don't ye mind ever having been here before?"

Thus questioned, Fred scanned his surroundings as best he could, but there was nothing that he could identify, and he so said, adding:

"I'm sure I've never been here before."

"And I'm sure ye have. This is the path that Lone Wolf come along, and that ye was hunting for when ye got lost, and fell into the basement story of the mountain."

"Oh, this is the pass, is it?" exclaimed the delighted lad; "then we have a clear road before us straight to New Boston."

"Clear of all but one thing."

"What's that?"

"The red spalpeens; they're always turning up when you don't expect 'em, and don't want 'em."

"How far are we away from the cave, where we left the half dozen Apaches?"

"I don't think it's much more than a mile, though it may be a mile and a half."

"Well, that's very good; we've got that much start, and it's worth having."

"And there's where ye're mistook, as the gals used to obsarve when anybody tried to run down my beauty. The path that we come along, ye'll mind, makes many turns and twists, and the ind of it all is that it strikes the pass on the other side of the cave, and we've got to ride right by the spot which we lift."

This was not cheering information, although, everything considered, the two had cause to congratulate themselves upon their extraordinary success up to this time.

The night was about gone, and, while their mustangs halted, they observed that it was growing light in the east. They would be forced to ride through the dangerous territory by day, so that the risk of detection would be proportionately greater if their enemies should be in the vicinity. Both the mustangs were fresh and vigorous, however, having enjoyed an unusually long rest, with plenty of food, and they were good for many hours of speed and endurance. The one ridden by Fred had behaved in a very seemly fashion, and there was ground for the hope that he would keep up the line of conduct to the end. Still there could be no certainty of what he would do in the presence of the Apaches.

"We'll take it aisy," said Mickey, as the two started off at an easy gallop. "We'll not be afther putting 'em to a run till we have to do the same, so that when there's naad for their spaad, we shall have it at command." This prudent suggestion was carried out. Their horses dropped into a sweeping gallop that was as easy as an ordinary walk. The riders kept their senses awake, talking only a little, and then in guarded voices.

As they galloped along the sun rose, and the day promised to be as warm and pleasant as those which had preceded it. The sky was obscured only by a few fleecy clouds, while the deep blue beyond was as beautiful as that of Italy. Drawing near the cave in the mountain, they pulled their horses down to a walk and carefully guided them into the softest places, so as to make the noise of their hoofs as slight as possible. Nothing occurred until they were a short distance beyond the dangerous spot, when Mickey spoke.

"Do you obsarve that stream there?" he asked, pointing to a rather deep brook which ran across the pass, and lost itself in the rocks upon the opposite side. "Well, that's the water that comes through the cave over the cascade, and that I expicted to swim out by, and I'm going to find out what me chances were."

CHAPTER XIII

IN THE NICK OF TIME

Leaving his mustang in charge of Fred, the Irishman turned to the right, and followed the stream into the rocks. The course was so winding that he speedily disappeared from sight. The boy, who was compelled to sit still and await his return, at perhaps the most dangerous portion of the road, felt anything but comfortable over the erratic proceeding of his friend. But, fortunately, the latter had been gone but a short time when he reappeared, hurrying forward as if somebody was at his heels.

"It's all right," he remarked, as he sprang into the saddle, took up the reins, and started on. "I think the Apaches are there, though I can't be sartin; but I found out what I wanted to l'arn."

Then he explained that he followed up the stream to the place where it came from beneath the rocks, which formed a part of the wall of the cave, where a curious fact attracted his attention. In its passage beneath the stone the tunnel widened and flattened, so that, where it shot forth to the sunlight again, its width was some twenty feet, and its depth only a few inches. The appearance it presented was very much like that of the gates of a mill-pond when they have been slightly raised to allow a discharge of water beneath. Through the passage-way thus afforded no living person could have forced his way; and, had Mickey O'Rooney attempted it, nothing in the world could have saved him from drowning. The Irishman himself realized it, and was thankful enough that he had refrained from making the desperate attempt.

The two continued their sweeping gallop for several hours, during which they did not catch a glimpse of Indians, but they were alarmed by hearing the reports of guns at no great distance on the right. The firing was irregular, sometimes several shots being heard together, and then they were more of a dropping character. This showed that a fight of some kind was going on, but as to its precise nature they could only conjecture. It might be that a party of Comanches and Apaches, or Kiowas, or hunters were enjoying a hot time, but the two friends were glad to get out of the neighborhood as speedily as possible. At noon they enjoyed the satisfaction of knowing that they had made good and substantial progress on the way home. There was an abundance of grass and water, and when the sun was overhead they went into camp.

"I'm as hungry as a panther that has been fasting for a month," said Mickey, as he dismounted; "and I haven't got a mouthful of food lift. There ain't any use of a chap starving to death to accommodate anybody else, and I don't mane to do the same."

Fred Munson's hunger was scarcely less than his, but the boy would have been willing to have undergone still more, rather than incur the risk that was now inevitable. But Mickey saw nothing to be gained by such a course and contended that they should give their attention to the wants of their bodies, before they were weakened by fasting and fatigue.

Mickey promised not to be absent long, and then started in

Lieut. R. H. Jayne

search of provender. Game was abundant in that part of the world, and he was confident that much time would not be required to bring down some toothsome dainty.

"He has an uncomfortable way of running off and leaving a fellow alone," muttered Fred, as he watched the vanishing figure of his friend. "I haven't anything but my revolver, and only two shots left in that, and it seems to me that this is about the worst place we could stop."

The point where they camped was in the pass, which, at that point, widened considerably. The right wall curved far inward in a semi-circular shape, the opposite remaining the same, the gorge looking as if an immense slice had been scooped out of its northern boundary. The rocks on every hand ranged from a dozen to a hundred feet in height, with numerous openings, through which a horseman could easily pick his way. The tops were covered with vegetation, the greater portion of which was vigorous and dense.

Fred found himself standing in an immense amphitheatre, as one can imagine how the gladiators of Rome stood in the Coliseum, when an audience of over a hundred thousand were seated and looking down upon them. He could not but note the helpless situation a party of men would be in if caught where he was.

"If a company of United States Cavalry should camp here, and the Indians opened on them from the rocks above, they would have to stand and be shot down, one after another, or else run the gauntlet and be picked off in the same way."

The appearance of the ground showed that the spot was a favorite camping-site of the Indians. Fred, for a time, suspected that it was the place where Lone Wolf and his band had spent the first night out from New Boston; but an examination showed that it did not correspond in many points. The remains of charred wood, of bleaching bones and ashes proved that many a camp-fire had been kindled. And, in all probability, every one of them had warmed the shins and toasted the food of the red cut-throats of that section.

The two mustangs were tethered near one side of the space where there was grass and water, and the lad set about it to select a proper place in which to build their camp-fire. There was no trouble in determining this; but, when he started to gather wood, he was surprised to discover that there was much less than he supposed. The former tenants of the place had cleared it up pretty thoroughly.

"There is plenty of wood over yonder," he said to himself, looking in the direction taken by Mickey O'Rooney; "and where there is so much growing there must be some upon the ground. I'll go over and gather some, and have the fire all ready when he comes back."

It was quite a walk from where he stood to the side of the semicircular widening of the pass, and as he went over it he was surprised to find it greater than it appeared. When he picked his way between the rocks, and began clambering among the trees and vegetation, he concluded that he was fully two hundred yards from where the mustangs were grazing.

However, he did not allow himself to lose any time in speculation and wonderment, but set to work at once to gather wood with which to kindle a fire in readiness for the return of Mickey. There was enough around him to afford all he needed and he was engaged in leisurely collecting an armful when he was startled by the rattling of the leaves behind him.

Lieut. R. H. Jayne

The wood was dropped on the instant, and the alarmed lad wheeled about to face his new danger. Instead of two or three Indians, as he had anticipated, he saw an enormous grizzly bear, about a dozen feet in the rear, coming directly toward him, with very little doubt of his purpose.

Fred had no thought of anything of this character, and for a time he was paralyzed with terror, unable to speak or stir. These precious seconds were improved by the huge animal, which continued lumbering heavily forward toward the boy. Bruin had his jaws apart and his red tongue lolling out, while a guttural grunt was occasionally heard, as if the beast was anticipating the crunching of the tender flesh and bones of the lad.

Before the latter was within reach, however, he had recovered his usual activity, and, with a bound and a yell of terror, Fred started in the direction of the clearing, where he had left the mustangs, and where he had intended to kindle the camp-fire. But the enormous, bulky creature, although swinging along in his awkward fashion, still made good speed, and gained so rapidly upon the boy that he almost abandoned hope of escape.

At this critical moment Fred thought of his revolver, and he whipped it out in a twinkling. Whirling about, he took quick aim and discharged both barrels almost in the face of the brute. Then, flinging the pistol against his leather nose, he turned back and continued his flight at the utmost bent of his speed. Both bullets struck the brute and wounded him, but not fatally, nor, indeed, enough to check his advance.

The grizzly bear, as found in his native wilds, is killed with extreme difficulty, and the only thing that seemed to affect the monster in the present instance was the flash of the pistol in his eyes. He paused, and, rearing on his hind legs, snorted, snuffed, and pawed his nose as if the bullets were splinters which he was seeking to displace. Then, with an angry growl, he dropped on all fours and resumed his pursuit of the author of his confusion and hurts. The wounds incensed the brute, and he plunged along at a faster rate than before, gaining so rapidly that there could be no doubt as to the result.

Being without any weapon at all, there seemed but one hope for Fred, and that was to reach his mustang in time to mount and avail himself of his speed. For a hundred feet or so he ran down a rapid slope, between the trees and rocks, until he reached the camping site, where he had a run of a couple of hundred yards across a comparatively level plain to reach the point where his animal was awaiting him.

In going down this wooded slope, the smaller size of the boy gave him considerable advantage. Yet, so well did the grizzly succeed that he reached the spot less than twenty feet in his rear, and, heading directly for him, at once proceeded to decrease the distance still further. This placed the question of escape by superior speed upon the part of the lad as among the impossibilities, and it began to look very much as if his race were run.

At this juncture, as if all the fates had combined against him, Fred, while glancing backward over his shoulder, stumbled and fell. He sprang up as hastily as possible, but the loss of ground was irreparable. As he looked back he saw that the colossal beast was so close that it seemed that one sweep of his paw would smite the terrified fugitive from the face of the earth.

It was a critical moment indeed, and the crack of the rifle from the wood, which the pursuer and pursued had just left, was not a breath of time too soon. Aimed by one who knew the vulnerable points of such a creature, and by someone whose skill was unsurpassed, the leaden messenger crashed its way through bone and muscle to the seat of life. The brute, which was ready to fall upon and devour the young fugitive, pitched heavily forward and rolled upon the ground in the throes of death.

Fred did not realize his delivery until he had gone some distance further and looked back and saw the black mass motionless upon the ground. After some hesitation, he then turned and walked distrustfully back to where it lay.

He found the beast stone-dead, a rill of blood from beneath the fore-leg showing where some one's bullet had done the business. The lad recalled the sound of the gun which had reached his ear.

"That was the best shot for me that Mickey ever made," he muttered, looking around for his friend.

But he was nowhere to be seen.

"Mickey must always have his fun," added Fred after failing to detect him. "Instead of coming out at once and letting me know how he came to do it, he fires the lucky shot, and then waits to see how I will act. My gracious! he is a bouncer!"

This last remark was excited by the carcass, which he kicked, and which shook like a mountainous mass of jelly; and as he passed around it he gained a fair idea of the immense proportions of the bear, in whose grasp he would have been as helpless as in that of a royal Bengal tiger.

"Whew! but he came mighty close to me! When I fell down I expected to feel his paws on me before I could get up. In a few seconds more it would have been all up with me."

Several minutes passed, and nothing was seen of the Irishman, whereupon the lad concluded he might as well go back and gather the wood, which would be needed at the camp-fire.

"I wonder if there's any more of them," he muttered, as he began picking his way among the rocks. "If there are, why Mickey must look out for me."

He found the sticks just as he had thrown them down and he proceeded to regather them, keeping a careful watch for another dangerous visitor. All remained quiet, however, and, making his way down the wooded slope into the open area, he looked back and found that he was still alone. So it continued until he returned to where the two mustangs were tethered. There he carefully adjusted the sticks and prepared everything, after which he began to feel some impatience at the non-appearance of his friend.

"He must see more fun in that kind of thing than I do. There's no telling what has become of those six Apaches we left down in the cave. I feel sure that they've got above ground again. It won't take long for them to find their mustangs, or some other horses, and they may be a mile away, and there may be other parties close by. Halloa!"

Fred thought that he had no matches about his person; but he was making a sort of aimless hunt when he found a solitary lucifer at the bottom of his pocket. This he carefully struck against the rock behind him, and in a few minutes the camp-fire was started and burning merrily.

As he sat down to wait he looked toward the point where the Irishman had vanished from sight. There he was, bearing on his shoulders some choice sections of a young antelope he had shot, although Fred recalled that he had not heard the report of his gun, except when the grizzly was shot. As Mickey came along over the same path taken by the boy, he was forced to make a detour around the carcass of the bear. He paused to survey it, his whole manner betraying great astonishment, as if he had never beheld anything of the kind. He walked around the body several times, punched it with his foot, and finally, grasping his twenty pounds of meat in his right hand, approached the camp-fire.

Here he at once began the preparations for broiling it. The antelope had been of goodly size and he had cut out the most luscious portions, so as to avoid carrying back any waste material. He had a great deal more than both could eat, it is true, but it was a commendable custom with the Irishman to lay in a stock against emergencies that were likely to arise.

While thus employed, it would have been impossible for Mickey to hold his tongue.

"Begorrah, but it was queer, was the same, the way I came to cotch this gintleman. I hunted him a little ways, when he made a big jump, and I thought had got a long ways off, but when I came to folly him, I found he had cornered himself among the rocks, where there was no show of getting out, except by coming back on me. The minute I showed mesilf, he made a rush for me arms, just as all the purty gals in Tipperary used to do when I came along the street. An antelope can't do much, but I don't care about their coming down on me in that style, and so I pulled up and let drive. He was right on me when I pulled trigger, and he made one big jump that carried him clear over my head, and landed him stone dead on the other side."

"That was a good shot, but not as good as when you brought down the grizzly bear at my heels."

Mickey O'Rooney was particularly busy just then with his culinary operations, and he stared at the lad with an expression of comical amazement that made the young fellow laugh.

"Begorrah, why don't ye talk sinse?" added Mickey, impatiently. "I've heard Soot Simpson say that if ye only put your shot in the right spot, ye don't want but one of 'em to trip the biggest grizzly that ever navigated. I was going to observe that ye had been mighty lucky to send in your two pistol-shots just where they settled the business, though I s'pose the haythen was so close on ye whin ye fired that ye almost shoved the weapon into his carcass."

"I shot him, Mickey, before I fairly started to run, but he didn't mind it any more than if I spit in his face. It was your own shot that did the business."

"Me own shot!" repeated Mickey, still staring with an astonished expression. "I never fired any shot at the baste, and never saw him till a few minutes ago, when I was coming this way."

It was Fred Munson's turn to be astonished, and he asked, in his amazed, wondering way:

"Who, then, fired the shot that killed him? I didn't."

"I thought ye did the same, for it was not mesilf."

The lad was more puzzled than ever. He saw that Mickey was in earnest, and was telling him the truth, and each, in fact, understood that *he* had been under a misapprehension as to who had slain the grizzly bear.

"The beast was right on me," continued Fred, "and I didn't

think there was any chance for me, when I heard the crack of a rifle from the bushes, and, looking back, saw that the bear was down on the ground, making his last kick."

Mickey let the meat scorch, while he stopped to scratch his head, as was his custom when he was in a mental fog.

"Begorrah, but that is queer, as me mither used to obsarve when she found she had not been desaved by belaving what we childer told her. There was somebody who was kind enough to knock over the grizzly at the most convanient season for ye, and then he doesn't choose to send over his card wid his post-office address on."

"Who do you think it was, Mickey?"

"It must have been some red spalpeen that took pity on ye. Who knows but it was Lone Wolf himself?"

Both looked about them in a scared, inquiring way, but could see nothing of their unknown friend or enemy, as the case might be.

"I tell you, Mickey, that it makes me feel as if we ought to get out of here."

"Ye're right, and we'll just swally some of this stuff, and then we'll 'light out."

He tossed the lad a goodly-sized piece of meat, which, if anything, was overdone. Both ate more rapidly than was consistent with hygiene, their eyes continually wandering over the rocks and heights around them, in quest of their seemingly ever-present enemies, the Apaches. It required but a few moments for them to, complete their dinner. Mickey, in accordance with his custom, carefully folded up what was left, and, taking a drink from the stream which ran near at hand, they sprang upon the backs of their mustangs, and headed westward in the direction of New Boston, provided such a settlement was still in existence by the grace of Lone Wolf, leader of the Apaches.

"Now," said Mickey, whose spirits seemed to rise when he found himself astride of his trusty mustang again, "if we don't have any bad luck, we ought to be out of the mountains by dark."

"And after that?"

"Then a good long ride across the prairie, and we'll be back again wid the folks."

"How glad I am that father isn't there, that he staid at Fort Aubray, for when he comes along in a few weeks, he won't know anything about this trouble till I tell him the whole story myself, and then it will be too late for him to worry."

"Yes, I'm glad it's so, for it saams if I had a spalpeen of a son off wid Lone Wolf, among the mountains, I'd feel as bad as if he'd gone in swimming where the water was over his head. And then it will be so nice to sit down and tell the ould gintleman about it, and have him lambaste ye 'cause you wasn't more respictful to Lone Wolf. All them things are cheerful, and make the occasion very plisant. Begorrah, I should like to know where that old redskin is, for Soot Simpson tells me that he is the greatest redskin down in this part of the world. He's the spalpeen that robbed a government train and made himself a big blanket out of the new greenbaeks that he stole. Soot says that there isn't room on his lodge-pole for half the scalps that he has taken. Bad luck to the spalpeen, he will peel the topknot from the head of a lovely woman, or swaat child, such as I used to be, as quick as he would from the crown of a man of my size. He's an old riprobate, is the same, and Soot says he can niver die resigned and at pace with all mankind till he shoots him."

"I'll be very glad to keep out of his way, if he'll keep out of mine. I wonder why he didn't kill me when he had the chance, instead of keeping me so long."

"I s'pose he meant to carry ye up where his little spalpeens live, and turn ye over to them for their amusement."

"How could I amuse them?"

"There be a good many ways. They might have stuck little wooden pegs in your hide, then set fire to 'em, and then walked ye round for fireworks; or they might fill your ears with powder, and tech it off, and then watched the iligant exprission of your countenance. Or they might lave set ye to running up and down between two rows of 'em, about eight or ten miles long, while aich stood with a big shillalah in his hand, and banged ye over the head with it as ye passed. There be a good many ways, according to what Soot told me, but that's enough to show ye that Lone Wolf and his folks wouldn't have been at a loss to find delightful ways of giving the little childher the innocent sport they must have."

"I shouldn't think they would, if that's the kind of fun they like," replied the horrified boy. "I've thanked the Lord hundreds of times that He helped me get out of Lone Wolf's clutches, and my dread is that he may catch us before we can get out of the mountain. I don't believe we could find as good a chance as I did the other night."

"Ye're right; that thing couldn't happen ag'in. Lightning doesn't strike twice in the same place; but we've got good horses, and if he don't pin us up in the pass, I think our chance is as good as could be asked."

"That's what troubles me," said Fred, who was galloping at his side, and who kept continually glancing from the tops of the rocks upon the right to the tops upon the left. "You know there are Indians all over, and I wonder that some of them haven't seen us already. S'pose they do, and they're behind us, they can signal to somebody ahead, and the first thing we know, they've got us shut in on both sides."

"That thing may happen," replied Mickey, who did not appear as apprehensive as his young friend; "but I have the best of hope that the same won't. I don't think Lone Wolf knows we're anywhere around here, and before he can find out, I also hope we shall be beyond his raich."

CHAPTER XIV

BETWEEN TWO FIRES

Mickey had scarcely given utterance to this hopeful remark when he drew up his mustang with a spasmodic jerk and exclaimed, in a startled in a startled voice:

"Do you see *that*?"

As he spoke, he pointed some distance ahead, where a faint, thin column of smoke was seen rising from the top of the rocks on the opposite side of the canon or pass.

It will be remembered that the pass of which our two friends availed themselves is the only one leading through the section of the mountains which lies to the eastward of the Rio Pecos. That part over which Fred and Mickey were riding showed numerous winding trails, made by the hoofs of the horses, as they passed back and forth, bearing Apaches, Comanches, Kiowas, and, very rarely, white men. At no very distant intervals were observed human skeletons and bones, while they were scarcely ever out of sight of the remains of horses or wild animals; all of which told their tale of the scenes of violence that had taken place in that highway of the mountains.

Sometimes war-parties of the tribes mentioned encountered each other in the gorge, and passed each other in sullen silence, or, perchance, they dashed together like so many wild beasts, fighting with the fury of a thousand Kilkenny cats. It was as the whim happened to rule the leaders.

The rocks rose perpendicularly on both sides to the height of fifty and a hundred feet, the upper contour being irregular, and varying in every manner imaginable. Along the upper edge of the pass grew vegetation, while here and there, along the side, some tree managed to obtain a precarious foothold, and sprouted forth toward the sun. The floor of the canon was of a varied nature—rocks, boulders, grass, streams of water, gravel, sand, and barren soil, alternating with each other and preventing anything like an accurate description of any particular section. A survey of this curious specimen of nature's highway suggested the idea that the solid mountain had been rent for many leagues by an earthquake, which, having opened this great seam or rent, had left it gradually to adjust itself to the changed order of things, and to be availed of by those who were seeking a safe and speedy transit through the almost impassable mountains.

Mickey and Fred checked their mustangs and carefully scrutinized the line of smoke. It was several hundred yards in advance, on their left, while they were following a trail that led close to the right of the canon. They could distinguish nothing at all that could give any additional information.

The fire which gave rise to the vapor had been kindled just far enough back to cause the edge of the gorge to protrude itself in such a way as to shut it off from the eyes of those below. Indeed, it was not to be supposed that those who had the matter in charge would commit any oversight which would reveal themselves or their purpose to those from whom they desired to keep them.

Lieut. R. H. Jayne

"That is the same as the camp-fire which troubled the three Apaches so much, and which was the means of my giving them the slip."

"It must have been started by some other war-party, so that their ca'c'lations were upsit, and you had a chance to get away during the muss. It was a sort of free fight, you see, in which, instead of staying and getting your head cracked, you stepped down and lift."

Unable to make anything of this particular signal-fire, the two friends carefully searched for more. Had they been able to discover one in the rear, they would have been assured that signaling was going on, and they would not have dared to venture forward. Here and there along the sides of the canon were openings or crevices, generally filled with some sort of a vegetable growth, and into most of which quite a number of men could have taken refuge, but which, of course, were inaccessible to their horses.

"I can't find anything that resimbles the same," said Mickey, alluding to the camp-fire, "though there may be some one that is seen by the gintlemen who are cooking their shins by yon one."

"Will it do to go on?"

"It won't do to do anything else. Like enough the spalpeen yonder has observed us coming, and he knows that there's a party behind us, and, being unable to do anything himsilf, he starts up the fire so as to scare us, and turn us back into the hands of the spalpeens coming in our rear. Mind, I say that such may be the case, but I ain't sure that it is."

"I shouldn't wonder a bit, now, if that isn't it exactly," said Fred, who was quite taken with the ingenious theory of his friend. "It seems to me that the best thing that we can do is to ride on as fast as we can."

"We've got to run the risk of it being all wrong, and fetching up in the bosom of the spalpeens; but it's moighty sure we don't make anything by standing here."

The Irishman turned his horse as near the middle of the canon as possible. Fred kept close to his side, his mustang behaving so splendidly that he gave him his unreserved confidence. The average width of the pass was about a hundred yards, so it will be understood that if a detachment of men were caught within it they would be compelled to fight at a fearful disadvantage.

The plan of Mickey and Fred, as they discussed it while riding along, was to keep up the moderate gallop until close upon the fire. They would then put their animals to the highest speed and pass the dangerous point as speedily as possible. They felt no little misgiving as they drew near the dangerous place, and they continually glanced upward at the rocks overhead, expecting that a party of Indians would suddenly make their appearance and open fire.

The first plan was, as they drew near, to run in as close as possible beneath the rocks on the left, in the belief that, as they overhung so much, the Indians above could not reach them with a shot. But before the time came to make the attempt, it was seen that it would not do. Accordingly, Mickey, who had maintained a line as close as possible to the centre of the canon, suddenly sheered his mustang to the right, until he nearly grazed the wall there. Then he put him on a dead run, Fred Munson doing the same, with very little space between the two steeds. A few plunges brought them directly opposite the signal-fire, and every nerve was strained.

　　　　　Lieut. R. H. Jayne

Both beasts were capable of magnificent speed and the still air became like a hurricane as the horsemen cut their way through it. Fred glanced upward at the crest of the rocks on the left and fancied that he saw figures standing there, preparing to fire. He hammered his heels against the ribs of his mustang and leaned forward upon his neck, in the hope of making the aim as difficult as possible.

Still no reports of guns were heard; and, after continuing the terrific gait for a quarter of a mile, they gradually decreased it until it became a moderate walk, and the riders again found themselves side by side. Both had looked behind them a dozen times since passing the dangerous point, but had not obtained a glimpse of an Indian.

"I thought I saw a number just as we were opposite," said Fred; "but, if so, what has become of them?"

"Ye didn't obsarve any at all, for I kipt raising me eye that way, and they weren't there. The whole thing is a moighty *puzzle*, as our tacher used to remark when the sum in addition became so big that he had to set down one number and carry anither. The spalpeens must have manufactured that fire for our benefit, and where's the good that it has done them?"

"Can't it be that it was for something else? Can't it be that they took us for Indians, or perhaps they haven't seen us at all, and don't know that we've passed?"

"It does seem as if something of the kind might be, and yet that don't sthrike me as the Injin style of doing business."

They continued their moderate pace for quite a distance further, continually looking back toward the camp-fire, the smoke from which continued to ascend with the same distinct regularity as before, but nothing resembling a warrior was detected. Finally a curve in the gorge shut out the troublesome signal, and they were left to continue their way and conjecture as much as they chose as to the explanation of what had taken place.

A little later, and when the afternoon was about half gone, they reached a portion of the pass which was remarkably straight, so that the eye took in a half mile of it, from the beginning to the point where another turn intervened. The two friends were galloping over this exact section and speculating as to how soon they would strike the open prairie, when all their calculations were knocked topsy-turvy. A party of horsemen charged around the bend in front, all riding at a sweeping gallop directly toward the alarmed Mickey and Fred, who instantly halted and surveyed them. A second glance showed them to be Indians, undoubtedly Apaches, and very probably Lone Wolf himself and some of his warriors.

"We must turn back," said the Irishman, wheeling his horse about and striking him into a rapid gait. "We've got to have a dead run for it, and I think we can win. Holy saints presarve us!"

This ejaculation was caused by seeing, at that moment, another party of horsemen appear directly in their front, as they turned on the back trail. Thus they were shut in on both sides, and fairly caught between two fires.

CHAPTER XV

ON THE DEFENSIVE

AT the moment of reining up their mustangs, the fugitives were about equidistant between the two fires, and it was just as dangerous to advance as to retreat. For one second the Irishman meditated a desperate charge, in the hope of breaking through the company that first appeared in his path, and, had he been alone, or accompanied by a man, he would have done so. But, slight as was his own prospect of escape, he knew there was absolutely none for the boy in such a desperate effort, and he determined that it should not be made.

"Can't we make a dash straight through them?" asked Fred, reading the thought of Mickey, as he glanced from one to the other, and noted the fearfully rapid approach of the redskins.

"It can't be done," replied the Irishman. "There is only one thing left for us."

"What is that?"

"Do as I do. Yonder is an opening that may serve us for awhile."

As he spoke, he slipped off his steed, leaving him to work his own will. Fred did not hesitate a moment, for there was not a moment to spare.

As he sprang to the ground, he pulled the beautiful Apache blanket from the back of the mustang that had served him so well. Dragging that with him, the two hurried to the right, making for a wooded crevice between the rocks, which seemingly offered a chance for them to climb to the surface above, if, in the order of things, they should gain the opportunity to do so. Mickey O'Rooney, as a matter of course, took the lead and in a twinkling he was among the gnarled and twisted saplings, the interlacing vines, and the rolling stones and rattling gravel. As soon as he had secured a foothold, he reached out his hand to help his young friend.

"Never mind me. I can keep along behind you. Go as fast as you can."

"Let me have the blanket," said Mickey, drawing it from his grasp. "Now come ahead, for we have got to go it like monkeys."

He turned and bent to his task with the recklessness of despair, for, even in that dreadful crisis, he thought more of the little fellow than he did of himself. If he could have been assured of his safety, he would have been ready to wheel about and meet his score or more of foes, and fight them single-handed, as Leonidas and his band did at Thermopylae. But the fate of the two was linked together, and, sink or swim, it must be fulfilled in company.

The narrow, wooded ravine, in which they had taken enforced refuge, was only three or four feet in width, the bottom sloping irregularly upward, at an angle of forty five degrees. So long as this continued, so long could they maintain their laboring ascent to the top. Mickey had strong hopes that, with the advantage of the start, they might reach that point far enough in advance of their pursuers to secure some other concealment that would serve them till nightfall, when they could steal out and try their chances again.

The saplings growing at every inclination afforded them much assistance, as they were able to seize hold with one or both hands, and thus help themselves along. But the vines in many places were of a peculiar running nature and they frequently caught their feet and stumbled; but they were instantly up and at it again. All at once Mickey, who was scarcely an arm's length in advance, halted so abruptly that Fred ran plump against him.

"Why don't you go on?" asked the panting lad.

"I can't. Here's the end."

So it was, indeed. While pressing forward with undiminished effort, the Irishman found himself suddenly confronted with a solid, perpendicular wall of rock. The narrow chasm, or fissure, terminated.

It was like a fugitive, his heart beating high with hope, checked in his flight by the obtrusion of the Great Chinese Wall across his path. Mickey looked upward. As he stood, he could, with outstretched arms, touch the wall on his right and left, and kick the one in front—the only open route being in the rear, which was commanded by the Apache party. As he did so, he saw, through the interstices of the interweaving, straggling branches, the clear, blue sky, with the edge of the fissure fully forty feet above his head. His first hope was that some of the saplings around him were lofty enough to permit him to use them as a ladder; but the tallest did not approach within a half dozen yards of the top. They were shut in on every hand.

"We can't run any further," said the Irishman, after a hasty glance at the situation. "We are cotched as fairly as ever was a mouse in a trap, and it now remains for us to peg away, and go under doing the best we can. Have ye your pistol?"

"Yes; I picked it up again, after throwing it in the face of the grizzly, but it isn't loaded."

"Then it ain't of much account, as me mither used to say in her affectionate references to me father; but if one of the spalpeens happen to come onto ye too suddent like, ye might scare him by shoving that into his eyes. I've got the powder for the same, but the bullets won't fit it, so I'll have to do the shooting."

They were at bay and the Irishman was right in his declaration that they could do nothing but fight it out as best they might. The question of further flight was settled by the trap in which they were caught.

They paused, expecting to hear the tramp of the Indians behind them, but, as it continued quiet, Mickey ventured upon a more critical inspection of their fortress, as it may be termed. He found little which has not already been mentioned, except the fact that the wall on their left sloped inward, as it ascended, to such a degree that the width at the top was several feet less than at the bottom. This was an important advantage, for, in case they were attacked from above, it was in their power to place themselves beyond the immediate reach of a whole war party by any means at their command.

"Do ye hear anything?" asked Mickey, bending his head to listen.

Lieut. R. H. Jayne

They were silent a few minutes, during which the occasional tramp of a horse's hoof was noted. Beyond a doubt, the entire war-party of Apaches were at the mouth of the fissure and probably a number had already entered it.

"They haven't tried to rush in pell-mell, head-over-heels," added Mickey, after they had stood thus a short time; but they are sneaking along, just as they always do when they're on the thrack of a gintleman."

"How soon do you think they will be here?" asked Fred, who had recovered his breath, and who began to feel something like a renewal of hope, faint though it might be, at the continued silence of their foes.

"Can't say, me laddy; but they may come any minute, and we must keep eyes and ears open, and be ready to do the last act in style. Don't ye mind that we're very much in the same fix that we was when cotched in the cave, barring that we're worse off here than we were there? If some one should let a lasso down from the top, we might climb up just as we did there; but that's one of the things that ain't likely to happen."

"Suppose we creep back a ways to see what the Indians are doing," ventured Fred, who was puzzled at the silence of their enemies, which had now continued for some time.

"No need of doing that just yet. They'll let us know what they're at and what they mane—whisht!"

At that juncture the Irishman detected a movement among the wood and undergrowth of the ravine, and his rifle was at his shoulder like a flash. Fred understood, or, rather, suspected, the cause of the trouble, though he saw nothing. Only a few seconds elapsed when the trigger was pulled. The sharp crack of the weapon had scarcely broke the stillness when the shriek of a warrior was heard only a few feet away, followed by a threshing of the vines and vegetation, as the comrades of the slain brave caught and hurriedly dragged him back toward the greater ravine beyond.

"That'll taich 'em to be more respictful in the traitment of gintlemen," remarked Mickey, who had recovered something of his natural recklessness, and was reloading his gun with as much *sangfroid* as though he had just dropped an antelope, and wished to be ready for another that was expected along the same path.

Fred had detected the rustling movement among the shrubbery made by the redskin in stealing upon them, but he saw nothing of the savage himself, and was not a little startled when his friend fired so quickly, and the result was so manifest.

If the victim of this rather hastily fired shot was unable to appreciate the lesson from its having a too personal application to himself, his companions appreciated it fully. It taught them that the way of pursuit was not open and undisputed by any means, and the few who were hurrying forward rather rashly were not only checked, but forced backward. Matters, for the moment, were brought to a stand still.

"They'll be back again," added Mickey, after reloading his piece, "and, as they mean to have our topknots, as the hunters say, we'll wipe out as many as we kin before they git them. And now, me laddy, will ye allow me to make a suggestion?"

"What is it?"

"That ye kaap a little more out of raich. If one of the spalpeens craap up, and shoots ye dead, ye'll be sorry ye didn't take me advice, when ye come to think the matter over coolly. Here's a sort of boulder which seems to have cared in from above. Do ye squaze in behind that."

"And what will you do?" asked Fred, acting upon his advice.

"Being as there isn't room to squaze in wid ye, I'll take my stand a little out here, where I can secure the protection of a similar piece of masonry, and where the spalpeens can't git by me without giving the countersign and showing a pass."

The lad did not specially like this arrangement, as it really retired him, but their quarters were so cramped that they had to dispose of themselves as best they could. He was obliged to feel that practically he was of no account, as his only pistol had become useless hours before. Accordingly, he forced himself in behind the boulder pointed out, and found that his position was safe against any treacherous shot from the front.

He was uneasy, however, about the open space above him, for it struck him that it would be so easy for any of their foes to roll the rocks down upon their heads. When he came to examine the situation more critically, he was not a little relieved to find that he was protected by the sloping wall, already mentioned. A heavy stone heaved over the opening above might really weigh a ton, and come crashing downward with terrific force, but no skill could, at the start, cause its course to be such as to injure the lad. He therefore concluded that his friend Mickey was not unwise in placing him in such a refuge.

CHAPTER XVI

FRIEND OR ENEMY?

It can scarcely be said that either of the fugitives had any definite hope of escape, for neither was able to see how the thing was possible. Mickey knew that occasionally, in the affairs of the world, seemingly providential interferences had occurred, but he looked for nothing of the kind. He considered that there would be a siege, lasting perhaps several days, then a desperate hand-to-hand struggle, and then.

The summary manner in which the Irishman disposed of the first Apache who showed himself brought matters to a standstill. In this condition they probably would have remained but for the Irishman himself, who saw nothing to be gained by inaction. Turning his head, he whispered to Fred:

"Do ye kape quiet, me laddy, till my return. I am going to take a look around."

The boy offered no objection, for he knew it would not be heeded, and Mickey moved away. It required the greatest care to pick his way down the fissure, as the stones and gravel were liable to turn under his feet and betray his approach, and it was much easier to go forward than backward.

The fissure which had afforded this temporary refuge was about fifty feet in length, and the vegetation was so thick that at almost any portion the view was no greater than three or four yards. Mickey was in constant expectation of encountering some of the Apaches at every step he took, and, in accordance with his principle of hitting a head wherever he saw it, he held his rifle so as to fire on the very instant the coppery face presented itself to view. But he saw none, and as he advanced he began to believe that the place was entirely free of the Apaches, who, if prudent, would quietly wait on the outside until their prey dropped into their hands.

It was not to be supposed that they would leave any opening on the outside by which the most forlorn chance could be obtained, and Mickey had no thought of any such thing. If he had, it would have been dissipated by the evidence of his own ears. He could hear distinctly their peculiar grunting voices, the tramp of their mustangs, and the evidence which a score of Indian warriors might be expected to give of their presence, when they had no reason for concealment.

"It may be that the spalpeens mean to make a rush upon me," he muttered, as he halted near the end of the fissure, "in which case I shall have a delightful employment in cracking their pates as they come up and take their turn."

He remained where he was a few minutes longer, and, seeing no prospect of learning anything additional, he resumed his advance until he reached a point where it was only necessary to draw the branches slightly apart to gain a view of the main ravine. And this he proceeded to do in the gentlest and most cautious manner possible.

The view was satisfactory, as it showed him that the Apaches were gathered at the entrance to the fissure and were taking matters very coolly and philosophically. Several were on horses, and a number on foot. Among the mustangs moving about, the Irishman recognized his own, astride of which was a dirty-looking Apache, with a wide mouth and broken nose.

"Ye ould spalpeen," muttered the indignant Irishman, "if it wasn't for fear of spoiling your wonderful booty, I'd turn you somersets off that hoss of mine, which I shall have to whitewash after getting him back, on account of your contact wid the same."

Mickey was strongly tempted to send a bullet after the tantalizing horse-thief, but he thought he could wait awhile. He was extremely cautious in making his stealthy view, only moving enough leaves to permit the service of his eyes and he had not enjoyed this prospect long before he believed that he had been detected.

Of the twenty-odd members comprising the Apache party, about a dozen were constantly in view, the others being too far to the right or left to be seen. The group was an irregular and straggling one, the most interesting portion being five or six, who stood close together, exactly at the base of the fissure, talking with each other. It was impossible that there should be more than one subject of discussion; and the dispute, as Mickey suspected, was as to the precise method of disposing of the job which had been placed in their hands.

Some, evidently, favored a daring charge directly up the narrow ravine, with its short, fierce encounter and sure victory. Others had a different plan, and their gestures led the eavesdropper to suspect that they advocated reaching them from the roof, while it was apparent that there were those who insisted upon waiting until the fruit should become ripe enough to fall into their laps without shaking. There could be little doubt that the Apaches preferred to take both prisoners, instead of shooting or tomahawking them in a fight. They were under the inspiration of Lone Wolf, who believed that a live man was much more valuable than a dead one.

While Mickey was watching this group with an interest which may be imagined, he noticed that a short, thick, greasy, filthy warrior was looking directly toward him, with a steadiness which caused the Irishman to suspect that his presence was known. The Indian, like all of them, was as homely as he could be. He, too, had gone through an attack of smallpox, which had left his broad face so deeply pitted that it could be noticed through the vari-colored paint which was daubed thereon. There was scarcely any forehead, the black, piercing eyes were far apart, and when Mickey saw them turned toward him, he felt anything but comfortable under their fire.

"I wonder whether he would keep mum if I should tip him the wink?" thought Mickey, who suffered the leaves in front of his face to close until there was just the smallest space through which he could watch his man.

The latter acted very much as if he suspected the proximity of the Irishman, even if he was not assured of it. He continued looking directly at the point where the eyes of the white man peered out upon him, and by-and-by he raised his arm and pointed in the same direction, saying something at the same time to a couple of the warriors near him.

"Be the powers, if that doesn't mane *me*, as me friend Larry O'Toole said when the judge axed for the biggest rascal in coort. I'll have to retire."

At this juncture a strange occurrence took place. Mickey

O'Rooney was looking straight at the man, when he saw him fling up his arms, yell and pitch forward to the ground, while the group instantly scattered, as if a bombshell had dropped at their feet.

Just a second previous to this strange death, Mickey heard the report of a rifle, showing that the warrior had been shot by some one at quite a distance from the spot, which shot, at the game time, caused a temporary panic among the others.

"Well, well, now, if that doesn't bate everything!" exclaimed the amazed Irishman. "Just as I was thinking of raising my gun to give that spalpeen his walking-papers, up steps some gintleman and saves me the trouble; *but who was the gintleman*? is the question."

The inexplicable occurrence naturally recalled Fred Munson's adventure with the grizzly bear. When he needed assistance most sorely, the shot was fired that saved his life. Could it be that the same party had interfered in the present instance? There was plenty of ground for speculation, and the Irishman was disposed to believe that the diversion came from some small party of Kiowas or Comanches, who had a special enmity against this company of Apaches, and who, being too weak to attack them, took this means of revenging themselves.

It was unsafe, however, to count upon the well-aimed shot as meant in the interest of the whites, although the one that brought down the grizzly bear could not have been meant for anything else than a direct help to the imperiled lad. The Southwest has been noted for what are termed "triangular fights." A party of Americans have been driven at bay by an overwhelming number of Mexicans or greasers, who have suddenly found themselves attacked by a party of howling Comanches. The latter have scattered the Mexicans like chaff, the Americans acting the part of spectators until the rout was complete, when the Comanches turned about and sailed into the Americans. The Kiowas, Comanches, Apaches, Mexicans and Americans afforded just the elements for a complication of guerilla warfare, in which matters frequently became mixed to a wonderful degree.

The hand that had fired this shot against a mortal foe of Mickey O'Rooney might be turned against him the next hour. Who could tell?

"If that gintleman begins the serenade from the other side, it's me bounden duty to kaap it up from this," concluded the Irishman, as he cocked his rifle and awaited his chance.

It was not long in coming. Only a few minutes had passed after the shot, when a couple of Apaches walked rapidly to view, and, approaching the remains of their comrade, stooped down to carry him away.

Mickey allowed them to get fairly started, when he blazed away at the foremost, and had the satisfaction of seeing the rear Apache not only deprived of his assistance, but his duty suddenly doubled. The warrior, however, stuck pluckily to the work, and dragged both out of view without any assistance from those who were ready to rush to his help.

These two, or rather three, rifle shots produced the strongest kind of effect upon the Apaches. They could not well fail to do so, for they were not only fired with unerring aim, but they came from such diverse points as to show the redskins that instead of having their enemies cooped up in this narrow ravine, they had, in one sense, placed themselves between two fires.

Hurriedly reloading his rifle, Mickey waited several minutes, determined to fire the instant he got the chance, with the purpose of enhancing the demoralization of the wretches. But they had received enough to teach them caution, and as the minutes passed, they failed to expose themselves. They had taken to shelter somewhere, and were not yet ready to uncover.

"When Mickey had waited a considerable time, he concluded to rejoin Fred Munson, who, no doubt, was anxious over the result of his reconnoissance. When he returned he found him seated upon the boulder, instead of behind it. The Irishman hastily explained what had taken place, and added:

"I don't know what they will do next, but we've give the spalpeens a dose that will kaap them in the background for a while."

"No, it won't, either," was the significant response.

"What do you maan, me laddy?"

"I mean that the Apaches, or some of them, anyway, have changed their base. I've heard something overhead that makes me sure they're up there, getting up some kind of deviltry."

CHAPTER XVII

A FORTUNATE DIVERSION

Mickey O'Rooney had not thought of the "opening" over their heads since the firing of his rifle-shot, and he now started and looked upward, as if fearful that he had committed a fatal oversight. But he saw or heard nothing to excite alarm.

"Where are they?" he asked, in a whisper.

"They're up there. I've seen them peep down more than once."

"What were they paaping for?"

"I suppose to find out where we were."

"Be the powers, but I showed them where I was when I fired me gun!"

"That maybe; but you didn't stay there, and perhaps they were looking for me."

"Did they find ye?"

"I don't think they did. You know I was in behind the boulder, with my head thrown back, so that it was easy for me to look up, and there wasn't enough branches and leaves over my head to shut out my view; so I lay there looking up, watching and listening, when I saw an Indian peep over the top there, as though he was looking for us."

"Did ye see more than one?"

"I am sure there were two, and I think three."

"They didn't ax ye any question?"

"I didn't hear any."

"What d'ye s'pose they mean to try?"

"I thought they meant to find out where we are hiding, and then roll stones down on us. They can do that, you know, without our getting a chance to stop them."

"If we squaze in under that same place," said Mickey, indicating the inward slope of the rock, they can't hit us; but I don't believe that such is their intention."

"What do you suppose it to be?"

"That's hard to say; but these varmints ain't ready to shoot us jist yet. Leastaways, they don't want to do so, until they're sure there ain't anything else lift for 'em to'do."

"They wish to make us prisoners?"

"That's it, exactly."

"Well, if they are willing to wait, they'll be sure to have us, for there isn't any water here for us to drink, and we can't get along without that."

The Irishman suddenly slapped his chest and side, as though he missed something from the pocket.

"And be the powers!" he exclaimed, "I've lost that mate, and there must have been enough to last us a wake or two."

"How could you have lost that?" asked Fred, who was much disappointed.

"It must have slid out when we were riding so hard, or else when we lift our horses."

"Are you sure it wasn't lost somewhere among these trees, where we can get it again?"

But he was confident that such was not the case, and he was not disposed to mourn the loss a great deal. They could do longer without food than they could without drink, and he was of the opinion that this problem would be solved before they were likely to perish from the want of either.

"Did ye get a fair look at any of the spalpeens that was so ill-mannered as to paap down on ye?"

"Yes; and there was one—'Sh! there he is now!"

The two peered upward through the leaves, and saw the head and shoulders of an Apache, who was looking down into the ravine. He was not directly above them, but a dozen feet off to the left. He seemed to be trying to locate the party that had fired two such fatal shots, and therefore could not have known where he was.

The face of the Indian could be seen very distinctly, and it was one with more individual character than any Mickey had as yet noticed. It was not handsome nor very homely, but that of a man in the prime of life, with a prominent nose—a regular contour of countenance for an Indian. The face was painted, as was the long black hair which dangled about his shoulders. His eye was a powerful black one, which flitted restlessly, as he keenly searched the ravine below.

Not seeing that which he wished, he arose to his feet, and walked slowly along and away from where the fugitives were crouching. That is, his face was turned toward the main ravine or pass, while he stepped upon the very edge of the fissure, moving with a certain deliberation and dignity, as he searched the space below for the man and boy whom he was so anxious to secure.

"I wonder if he ain't the leader?" said Mickey, in a whisper. "I never saw better shtyle than that."

"I should think he was the leader. Don't you know him?"

"How should I know him? I never traveled much in Injun society. Are ye and him acquainted?"

"He's Lone Wolf—their great war-chief."

"Ye don't say so?" exclaimed the astonished Irishman, staring at him. "He's just the spalpeen I loaded me gun for, and here goes!"

Softly raising the hammer of his rifle, he lifted the weapon to his shoulder; but before he could make his aim certain, the red scamp stepped aside and vanished from view.

"Now, that's enough to break a man's heart!" wailed the

chagrined Mickey. "Why wasn't the spalpeen thoughtful and kind enough to wait until I could have made sartin of him? But sorra and disappointment await us all, as Barney Mulligan said when his friend wouldn't fight him. Maybe he'll show himsilf agin."

Whether or not Lone Wolf learned of the precise location of the parties for whom he was searching can only be conjectured; but during the ten minutes that Mickey held his weapon ready to shoot him at sight, he took good care to keep altogether invisible.

The Irishman was still looking for his reappearance, when another singular occurrence took place. There was a whoop, or rather howl, followed by a fall of a warrior, who was so near the edge of the narrow ravine that when he came down, a portion of his body was seen by those below. The dull and rather distant report of a gun told the curious story.

The same rifle that had picked off one of the Apaches at the mouth of the fissure had done the same thing in the case of one at the top. The aim in both instances was unerring.

"Freddy, me lad," said Mickey, a moment later, "whin we rushed in here wid the spalpeens snapping at our heels, I hadn't any more hope that we'd ever get clear of 'em than the man who was transported to Botany Bay had of cutting out Prince Albert in Queen Victoria's graces."

"Have you any more hope *now*?"

"I have; we've got a friend on the outside, and he's doing us good sarvice, as he has already proved. If Lone Wolf wasn't among that crowd, I don't belave they would stay after what has took place; there's nothing to scare an Injun like them things which he don't understand."

"I should think that that rifle-shot is proof enough that somebody is firing into them."

"Be the powers, but ye know little of Injin devilments, as I've larned 'em from Soot Simpson. How do ye know but that's a thrick to make these Apaches belave that there's but a single Kiowa over there popping at them, when there may be half a hundred waiting for the chance to clean them out?"

"Maybe that is Sut himself; you know you have been expecting him."

"It can't be him," replied Mickey, with a shake of his head. "He would have showed himself long ago, when he could be sure of helping us. There must be some redskins over there that have put up a job on Lone Wolf and his scamps."

"Whoever it is, whether one or a dozen, they are helping us mightily."

"So it looks, though they don't mean it for that, and after driving these spalpeens away, they may come over to clean us out themselves."

Nothing was heard of the redskins above for a considerable time after the shot mentioned. Then the body was suddenly whisked out of sight. It is a principle with Indians to bring away their dead from any fight in which they may have fallen. At the imminent risk of losing his own life a warrior had stolen up and drawn away the remains of his former comrade.

The mysterious shots seemed to come from the other side of the ravine, and they naturally had a very demoralizing effect upon the party. Lone Wolf was not only brave, but sagacious and prudent. He was not the chief to allow his warriors to stand idly and permit themselves to be picked off one by one by an unseen enemy. But for the latter, he would have descended into the fissure, and, with several of his most reliable braves, captured and secured Mickey and his companion at all hazards. But what assurance could he have that after he and his men had entered the little ravine, a whole party of Kiowas would not swarm in, overwhelm them, and make off with their horses? So the leader concluded for the time being to remain outside, where his line of retreat would be open, while he could arrange his plans for disposing of the whites at his leisure.

Lone Wolf dispatched two of his most skillful scouts, one to the right, the other to the left, with orders to get to the rear of the enemy, no matter how long a detour was necessary. In case they were unable to extinguish them, they were to signal or return for assistance. After sending off his trusty messengers, Lone Wolf concluded to hold back until their return, keeping himself and his braves pretty well concealed, but guarding against the capture of their horses in the ravine below, or the escape of the two fugitives, who might attempt to take advantage of the diversion.

At the end of an hour, nothing had been seen or heard of the Apache scouts sent out, and the chief dispatched another to learn what was going on, and what was the cause of the trouble. During this hour not a rifle-shot was detected by the waiting, listening ears. Another half hour passed away, and the third man sent out by Lone Wolf came back alone, and with astounding tidings.

He had found both of the warriors lying within a few yards of each other, stone dead. He sought for some explanation of the strange occurrence, but found none, and returned with the news to his leader.

The latter was about as furious as a wild Indian could be, without exploding. Lone Wolf had his own theory of the thing, and he inquired particularly as to the manner in which the fatal wounds seemed to have been inflicted. When they were described, all doubt was removed from the mind of the chieftain.

He knew where the fatal shots came from, and he determined that there was no better time to "square accounts." Calling the larger portion of his company about him, he started backward and away from the ravine, his purpose being to reach the rear of his enemy by a long detour.

Lieut. R. H. Jayne

CHAPTER XVIII

AN OLD ACQUAINTANCE

All this was grist for Mickey and Fred. The long silence and inaction—so far as these two were concerned—of the Apaches convinced the fugitives that some important interruption was going on, and that it could not fail to operate in the most direct way in their favor. It was well into the afternoon when the collision occurred between them and the Apaches, and enough time had already passed to bring the night quite close at hand. An hour or so more, and darkness would be upon them.

"I don't belave the spalpeens have found put just the precise spot where we've stowed away," said Mickey, in his cautious undertone, to his companion, "for I've no evidence that such is the case."

"They may take it into their heads to come into the fissure again, and then where are we?"

"Right here, every time. We couldn't get a better spot, unless it might be at the mouth."

"Don't you think we had better go there?" asked the lad, who could not feel the assurance of his friend.

"I see nothing to be gained by the same, as Tim O'Loony said when some one told him that honesty was the best policy. If we start to return there, they'll find out where we are, and begin to roll stones on us. I don't want to go along, dodging rocks as big as a house, wid an occasional rifle-shot thrown in, by way of variety."

"Don't you fear they will creep in and try to surprise us?"

"Not before dark, and then we can shift our position."

"Do you believe there is any hope at all for us in the way of getting out?"

The Irishman was careful not to arouse too strong hopes in the breast of the lad, and he tried to be guarded in his reply:

"An hour ago I would have sworn if there war a half-dozen of us in here, there was no show of our getting away wid our top-knots, for the raison that there is but one hole through which we could sneak, and there's twenty of 'em sitting round there, and watching for us; but I faal that there is some ground for hope."

"What reason for your saying there is hope? Isn't it just as hard to get out the front without being seen?"

"It might be just now; but there's no telling what them ither spalpeens mane to do arter the sun goes down. S'pose they get Lone Wolf and his men in such a big fight that they'd have their hands full, what's to hinder our sneaking out the back-door during the rumpus, hunting up our mustangs, or somebody else's, and resooming our journey to New Boston, which these spalpeens were so impertinent as to interrupt a short time since?"

Fred Munson felt that this was about as rose-colored a view as could be taken, and indeed a great deal rosier than the situation warranted—at least, in his opinion.

"Mickey, if that isn't counting chickens before they're hatched, I don't know what is! While you're supposing things, suppose these Indians don't do all that, where's going to come our chance of creeping out without their knowing it?"

Mickey scratched his head in his puzzled way, and replied:

"I'm sorry to obsarve that ye persist in axing knotty questions, as I reproved me landlord for doing in the ould country, when he found me digging praities in his patch. There's a good many ways in which we may get a chance to craap out, and I'm bound to say there be a good many more by which we can't; but the good Lord has been so good to us, that I can't help belaving He won't let us drop jist yet, though He may think that the best thing for us both will be to let the varmints come in and scalp us."

There was a good deal of hope in the Irishman, and a certain contagion marked it, which Fred Munson felt, but he could not entertain as much of it as did his older and more experienced friend. Still, he was ready to make any attempt which offered the least chance of flight. He was hungry and thirsty, and there was no way of supplying the wants, and he dreaded the night of suffering to be succeeded by the still more tormenting day.

It was very warm in the ravine, where not a stir of air could reach them. If they suffered themselves to be cooped up there through the night, they would be certain to continue there during the following day, for it was not to be expected by the wildest enthusiast that any way of escape presented itself under the broad sunlight. The following night must find them more weakened in every respect; for the chewing of leaves, while it might afford temporary relief, could not be expected to amount to much in a run of twenty-four hours. Clearly, if anything at all was to be done or attempted, it should not be deferred beyond the evening, which was now so close at hand.

But the objection again came up that whatever Mickey and Fred decided on, hinged upon the action of parties with whom they had nothing to do, and with whom, as a matter of course, it was impossible to communicate. If the Kiowas, as they were suspected to be, should choose to draw off and have nothing further to do with the business, the situation of the fugitives must become as despairing and hopeless as in the first case.

There perhaps was some reason for the declaration of Mickey that the strangers (their allies for the time being) were a great deal more likely to perform their mission before the sun should rise again. Consequently, the next few hours were likely to settle the question one way or the other.

"Do you know whether any of the Apaches are still up there?" asked Fred.

"Yes; there be one or two. I've seen 'em since we've been talking, but they're a good deal more careful of showing their ugly faces. They paap over now and then, and dodge back agin, before I can get a chance to pop away."

"Would you try and shoot them if you had the chance?"

"Not just yet, for it would show 'em where we are, and they would be likely to bother us."

The two carried out this policy of keeping their precise

location from the Indians so long as it was possible, which would have been a very short time, but for the terror inspired among the Apaches from the shots across the pass. Mickey had no suspicion that Lone Wolf and his best warriors were absent on a hunt for the annoying cause of these shots. Had he known it, he might have been tempted upon a reconnoissance of his own before sunset, and so it was well, perhaps, that he remained in ignorance.

Within the next hour night descended, and the ravine, excluding the rays of the moon, became so dark that Mickey believed it safe to venture out of their niche and approach the pass, into which they had no idea of entering until the ground had been thoroughly reconnoitered.

"The spalpeens will be listening," whispered Mickey, as they crept out, "and so ye naadn't indulge in any whistling, or hurrahing, or dancing jigs on the way to our destination."

Fred appreciated their common peril too well to allow any betrayal through his remissness. Favored by the darkness, they crept carefully along over the rocks and boulders, and through the vines and vegetation, until they were so close that the man halted.

"Do ye mind and kaap as still as a dead man, for we're so close now that it won't do to go any closer till we know what the spalpeens are doing."

The two occupied this position for some time, during which nothing caught their ears to betray the presence of men or animals. Feeling the great value of time, Mickey was on the point of creeping forth, when he became aware that there was somebody moving near him. The sound was very slight, but the proof was all the more positive on that account; for it is only by such means that the professional scout judges of the proceedings of a foe near him.

His first dread was that the individual was in the rear, having entered the fissure while they were at the opposite end, and then allowed them to pass by him. But when the faint rustling caught his ear again there could be no doubt that it was in front of him.

"One of the spalpeens—and maybe Lone Wolf himself—coming in to larn about our health," was his conclusion, though the situation was too critical to allow him to communicate with the lad behind him.

Reaching his hand back, he touched his arm, as a warning for the most perfect silence.

The boulder against which he was partly resting was no more quiet and motionless than Fred, who had nerved himself to meet the worst or best fortune. A few minutes more listening satisfied Mickey that the redskin was not a dozen feet in front, and that a particularly large boulder, which was partly revealed by some stray moonlight that made its way through the limbs and branches, was sheltering the scout. Not only that, but he became convinced that the Indian was moving around the left side of the rock, hugging it and keeping so close to the ground that the faintest shadowy resemblance of a human figure could not be detected.

It was at this juncture that the Irishman determined upon a performance perfectly characteristic and amusing in its originality. Carefully drawing his knife from his pocket, he managed to cut a switch, some five or six feet in length, the end of which was slightly split. He next took one of his matches, and struck it against the rock, holding and nursing the flame so far down behind it that not the slightest sign of it could be seen from the outside. Before the match had cleared itself of the brimstone, Mickey secured the other end of the stick in his hand. His next proceeding was to raise this stick, move it around in front, and then suddenly extend it at arms length. This brought the burning match into the dense shadow alongside the rock, and directly over the head of the amazed scout. The Hibernian character of the act was, that while it revealed to him his man, it also, although in a less degree, betrayed the location of Mickey himself, whose delighted astonishment may be imagined, when, instead of discerning a crouching, painted Apache, he recognized the familiar figure of Sut Simpson, the scout.

"What in thunder are ye driving at?" growled the no less astonished Sut, as the flame was almost brought against his face. "Do yer take me for a kag of powder, and do ye want to touch me off?"

"No, but I was thinking that that long, red nose of yourn was so full of whiskey that it would burn, and I wanted to make sartin."

CHAPTER XIX

HOW IT WAS DONE

From the very depths of despair, Mickey O'Rooney and Fred Munson were lifted to the most buoyant heights of hope.

"I always took yer for a hoodlum," growled the scout; "but you've just showed yerself a bigger one than I s'posed. Yer orter fetched a lantern with yer, so as to use nights in walking round the country, and looking for folks."

"Begorrah, if that isn't the idaa!" responded the Irishman, with mock enthusiasm; "only I was considering wouldn't it be as well to call out the name of me friends. Ye know what a swate voice I have. When I used to thry and sing in choorch, the ould gintleman always lambasted me for filing the saw on Sunday. But why don't ye craap forward and extend me yer paw, as the bear said to the man?"

Sut, however, did not move, but retained his crouching position beside the large boulder, speaking in the lowest and most guarded voice:

"It won't do; we haven't any time to fool away yerabouts. Is that younker wid yer?"

"Right at me heels, as me uncle concluded when the bulldog nabbed him."

"Come ahead, then. Shoot me! but this ain't a healthy place to loaf in just now. The 'Paches are too plenty and too close. We must light out."

"Sha'n't I shtrike anither match to *light* us out by?"

"Hold your tongue, will you? Creep right along behind me, without making any noise at all, and don't rise to your feet till yer see me do it, and don't open your meat-traps to speak till I axes yer a question, if it isn't till a month from now. Do yer understand me?"

Mickey replied that he had a general idea of his meaning, and he might as well go ahead with the circus. Fred had caught the whispered conversation, and, of course, knew what it meant. As Mickey turned round to see where he was, he found him at his elbow.

"Sh! Come ahead, now. We're going to creep straight across the pass till we reach t'other side, when we'll go down that some ways, and I'll tell yer the rest."

A second or two afterward the long, wiry frame of the scout emerged from the dense shadow at the side of the boulder, and crept forward in the direction of the middle of the main ravine or pass. Close behind him followed Mickey and Fred, the trio forming a curious procession as they carefully picked their way across the moonlit gorge, the grass for most of the distance being so dense that they were pretty well screened from view.

The directions of the scout were carefully obeyed to the letter, for, indeed, there could have been no excuse for disregarding them. He understood perfectly the nature of the task he had undertaken, and the risk he ran was entirely for the benefit of his friends.

One of the first and most important requisites of a scout is patience, without which he is sure to commit all manner of errors. In the present case, it seemed to Fred that much valuable time could be saved if they would simply rise to their feet and make a dash straight across the ravine. Even Mickey was of the same opinion, at least to the extent of varying the pace so as to go slowly part of the time and rapidly the rest, as the ground became unfavorable or favorable. But it was very clear that Sut Simpson held very different views.

A piece of machinery could not have advanced with a more regular movement than did he—a movement that was excessively trying to an impatient person who could not understand his reason for it. Mickey could see that he turned his head from side to side, and was using his eyes and ears to the extent of their ability. At the end of some fifteen or twenty minutes the base of the perpendicular wall on the opposite side was reached, and, greatly to the relief of his companions, he arose to his feet, they following suit.

"Begorrah, but that's a swate relief, as me Aunt Bridget observed, when her ould man."

A turn of the head, and an impatient gesture from the scout, silenced Mickey before he had time to complete the remark. He subsided instantly, and began a debate with himself as to whether he ought not to apologize for his forgetfulness, but he concluded to wait.

The long, lank figure of Sut Simpson looked as if it was a shadow slowly stealing along the dark face of the rock, followed by that of Mickey and the lad. They were as silent as phantoms, each walking as tenderly and carefully as though he was a burglar breaking into the house of some sleeping merchant, whose slumbers were as light as down. Mickey had no doubt that this was continued twice as long as necessary, although he conscientiously strove to carry out the wishes of the scout in that respect. He stumbled once or twice, but that was because of the treacherous nature of the ground.

They must have journeyed fully a quarter of a mile in this fashion before Sut held up in the least. During all this time, so far as Mickey could judge, nothing had been seen or heard of the Apaches, who, supposedly, would have guarded the outlet, in which the two had taken refuge, with a closeness that could not have permitted such an escape; but not one had been encountered.

It was a most extraordinary occurrence all through, and Mickey found it hard to understand how one man, skilled and brave though he was, could perform such a herculean task, for there could be no doubt that to him, under Providence, belonged the exclusive credit. Of course it was Sut who had fired the shot that saved Fred from a terrible death by the grizzly bear, and his well aimed and opportune shots had done the fugitives inestimable service when they were crouching in the fissure and despairing of all hope. But there must have been something back of all this. The scout must have possessed a greater power, which had not become manifest to his friends as yet.

"Now yer can walk with more ease," he said, as he dropped back beside his companions; "but, at the same time, don't talk too loud. Let us all keep as much in the shadder as we kin, for there may be other varmints around, and there's no telling when you're likely to run agin 'em."

"But where are the spalpeens that shut us up in that split in the rocks?"

"They're all behind us, every varmint of them, and thar they're likely to stay for awhile; but, Mickey, I want yer to tell me what happened arter we parted among these mountains, and took different routes far the younker here."

The Irishman related his experience in as brief a manner as possible, the scout listening with a great deal of interest, and asking a question or two.

"The luck was yer's," he said, when the narrator concluded, "of gettin' on the right track, while I got on the wrong."

Mickey scratched his head in his old quizzical way.

"The same luck befell the spalpeens and mesilf. I first got on their thrack, and then they got on mine, so we'll call that square, as Mike Harrigan did when he went back the second night and took the other goat so as to make a pair."

"That was nigh onto a bad fix when yer pitched into that cave, and couldn't find the way out till the wolf showed the younker; but it wasn't so bad as yer think, 'cause I'd been sure to find yer war thar. I know the way in and out of it, and I could have got into it and fetched you out, but yer war lucky 'nough not to need me."

"How was it that ye were so long turning up arter we separated?"

"Wal, Lone Wolf and his braves rode so fast that it was a good while afore I cotched up, and found that he hadn't the younker with him. Then, in course, I turned back and found that yer had flopped so much, off and on yer trail, that there was a good deal of trouble to keep track of yer."

"Where did ye first catch the light of Mickey O'Rooney's illegant and expressive countenance?"

"I saw yer stop to camp this morning a good ways up the pass, whar yer cooked yer piece of antelope meat, and swallowed enough to last yer for a week."

"It was you that shot the grizzly bear just as he was going to kill me?" inquired Fred, with a pleased look in the scarred face of the scout, who smiled in turn as he answered:

"I have a 'spicion it war me and nobody else."

"Why didn't ye come forward and introduce yerself?" inquired Mickey, "it was all a mistake to think that we felt too proud to notice ye, even if ye ain't as good-looking as meself."

"Wal, I thought I'd watch yer awhile, believing I could do yer more service than by jining in, as was showed by what took place arterwards. Whar would yer have been if I'd got shet up in that trap with yer? Lone Wolf would've had our ha'r long ago."

"But how did ye manage to fool the pack into giving us a chance to craap out?"

"That was easy enough when yer understand it."

"I thought it would come aisier to a man who understood how to do it than it did to one who didn't know anything about it."

"Arter picking off one or two of the varmints, that made

Lone Wolf mad, and he sent out a couple of his warriors to wipe me out. He didn't think I knowed his game, but I did, and when they got round to where I was I just slid 'em under afore they knowed what the matter was. When he sent a third varmint arter them, and he went back and told the chief that the first two had gone to the eternal hunting grounds, he was so all-fired mad that he left only a half dozen to watch the hole where you was to come out, while he took the rest and come arter me."

"I know a good many of Lone Wolf's signals," added the scout, with a chuckle, "and arter he had been on this side for a while, I dipped down into the pass, and signaled for the rest of 'em to come. They come, every one of 'em, and then I went for you, not certain whether yer war mashed or not. We got away in good time to save ourselves running agin 'em."

Lieut. R. H. Jayne

CHAPTER XX

SUT'S CAMP FIRE

"But where are Lone Wolf and his warriors?" asked Fred.

"Back yonder somewhere," replied the scout, indifferently. "They came over into the woods this side the pass to look for the Kiowas that have been picking off thar warriors. It'll take 'em some time to find the varmints, I reckon."

"It's mesilf that would like to ax a conundrum," said Mickey, "provided that none of the gintlemin prisent object to the same."

Sut gave the Irishman to understand that he was always pleased to hear any inquiry from him, if he asked it respectfully.

"The question is this: How long are we to kape thramping along in this shtyle? Is it to be for one wake or two, or for a month? The raison of me making this respictful inquiry is that the laddy and mesilf have become accustomed to riding upon horses, and it goes rather rough to make the change, as Jimmy O'Brien said when he broke through the ice and was forced to take a wash, arter having done without the same thing for several months."

This gentle intimation from Mickey that he preferred to ride was promptly answered by the scout to the effect that his own mustang was some distance away in the wood, but he was unable to locate either of theirs, which they abandoned at the time they took such hurried refuge in the narrow ravine.

"But what become of all the craturs?" persisted Mickey, who was anything but satisfied at this plodding along. "Lone Wolf and his spalpeens did not ride away upon their horses."

"No, but yer may skulp me if any of 'em are big enough fools to leave their animals where there seems to be any danger of other folks layin' hands on 'em. When the rest of his band come over arter him, as they s'posed in answer to their signal, they took mighty good care not to leave their hosses where thar war any chance for the Kiowas to put their claws onto 'em. They rode off up the pass till they could reach a place whar the brutes could climb up and jine thar owners."

"Then I'm to consider the question settled," responded Mickey, "and we're to tramp all the way to New Bosting, ef the place is still standing. Av coorse we can do the same, which I take to be three or four thousand miles, provided we have the time to do it and ain't disturbed."

Sut, after permitting his friend to hold this opinion for a time, corrected it in his own way.

"Thar ain't no use of tryin' to reach home on foot, any more than thar is of climbing up that wall with yer toes. Arter we strike camp, we'll stop long enough to eat two or three bufflers, and rest, and while yer at that sort of biz, I'll 'light out, and scare up something in the way of hoss flish. Thar's plenty of it in this part of the world, and a man needn't hunt long to find it. Are ye satisfied Mickey?"

Lieut. R. H. Jayne

The Irishman could not feel otherwise, and he expressed his profound obligations to the scout for the invaluable services he had already rendered them.

"Lone Wolf knows me," said Sut, making a rather sudden turn in the conversation. "Me and him have had some tough scrimmages years ago, as I was tellin' that ar Barnwell, or Big Fowl, rather, that has had the charge of starting the place called New Boston. I've got 'nough scars to remember him by, and he carries a few that he got from me. I have a style of sliding his warriors under, when I run a-foul of 'em, that Lone Wolf understands, and he's larned long ago who it was that wiped out them two varmints that he sent out to look around arter me. Halloa! here we air!"

As he spoke, he reached a break in the continuity of the wall to which they had been clinging. The opening was somewhat similar to that into which Mickey and Fred had been driven in such a hurry, except that it was broader and the slope seemed more gradual.

Simpson turned abruptly to the left, and they began clambering upward. It took a considerable time to reach the level, and when they did so the scout led them back to the edge of the pass, which wound along fifty or a hundred feet below them.

"Thar's whar we've come from," said he, as they looked down in the moonlit gorge; "and while that's mighty handy at times, yet it's a bad place to get cotched in, as yer found out for yerselves."

"No one will dispoot ye, Soot, especially when Lone Wolf and a score of spalpeens appears in front of ye, and whin ye turn about to lave, ye find him and a dozen more in your rear. That was a smart thrick was the same; but if he hadn't showed himsilf in both places at the same time, we would have stood a chance of giving him the slip, as we had good horses under us."

"Can't always be sartin of that. Them varmints have ways of telegraphing ahead of ye to some of thar friends, so that ye'r'll run heels over head into some trap, onless yer understands thar devilments and tricky ways."

"When we were in camp," said Fred, "we saw the smoke of a little fire near by. Was it yours?"

"It war," replied Sut, with a curious solemnity. "I kindled that fire, and nussed it."

"Well, it bothered us a good deal. We didn't know what to make of it, Mickey and I."

"It bothered the varmints a good deal more, which war what it war intended for. I meant it far a Kiowa signal-fire, and if it hadn't been started 'bout that time, you'd had some other grizzly b'ars down on ye in the shape of 'Paches."

"But it didn't help us all the way through; they came down on us a little while afterward."

"That war accident," said Sut. "the purest kind of accident— one of them things that is like to happen, and which we don't look for—a kinder of surprise like."

"As me father obsarved when he found we had twins in the family," interrupted Mickey.

"The chances are ten to one that thing couldn't happen ag'in; but luck, just then, war t'other way. Lone Wolf and his men war on their way home, and had no more idea of meeting yer folks than he had of axing me to come down and act as bridesmaid for his darter, when she gits married."

"Do ye s'pose he knowed us, Soot?" asked the Irishman.

"It isn't likely that he did at first, but the sight of the younker must have made him 'spicious, and arter he rammed you into the rocks, I guess he knowed pretty well how things stood, and he war bound to have both of yer."

"What made him want *me* so bad?" asked Fred. "I never understood how that was."

The tall scout, standing on the edge of the broad, deep ravine, looked down at the handsome face of the boy, to whom he felt attracted by a stronger affection than either he or the Irishman suspected.

"Bless your soul, my younker, that ere Lone Wolf that they call such a great chief (and I may as well own up and say that he is), is heavy on ransoms and he ain't the only chief that's in that line. That skunk runs off with men, women and boys, and his rule is not to give 'em up ag'in till he gits a good round price. He calculated on making a good thing off you, and I rather think he would."

"Does he always give up those, then, that their friends want to ransom?"

"Not by any means; it's altogether as the notion takes him. He sports more skulps and topknots than any of his brother-chiefs, and he never lets his stock run low. As them other varmints creep up onto him, he shoots ahead by scooping in more topknots, and thar's no use of thar trying to butt ag'in him. He's 'way ahead of 'em, and there he's bound to stay, and they can't help it."

"Then he might have used me the same way, after all the pains he took to get me."

"Jest as like as not. He is as ugly as the devil himself. Two years ago he stole a good-looking gal up near Santa Fe. He had a chance for the biggest kind of ransom; but the poor gal had long, golden hair, and the skunk wanted it for an ornament, and he took it, too, and thinks more of it than any out of his hundred and more. Arter getting yer home among his people, and arter he'd found out thar's a good show fur a big ransom from yer father, jest as like as not he'd make up his mind that the best thing he could do would be to knock ye on ther head and raise yer ha'r, and he'd do it, too."

"Well, thank heaven, none of us are in his hands now, and I pray that he may never get us."

The three were still standing as close to the edge of the ravine as was prudent, so that the moonlight fell about them. They were enabled to see quite a long distance up and down the pass, the uncertain light, however, causing objects to assume a fantastic contour, which would have made an inexperienced person uncertain whether he was looking down upon animate or inanimate objects. They were on the point of moving away, when Fred Munson exclaimed, with some excitement:

"The country seems to be full of camp-fires or signal-fires. Yonder is one just started!"

He pointed up the ravine, and to the other side, where an unusually bright star seemed to be rising over the solitude beyond. It was about a quarter of a mile away, and its brightness such as to show its nature.

"Yes, that's one of 'em," said the scout, in a tone which

showed that he had no particular interest in it.

"Can ye rade what the same manes?" asked Mickey, who was gradually accumulating a wonderful faith in the woodcraft of the scout.

But the latter laughed. It would have been the height of absurdity for him to have pretended that he could make anything of the meaning of a simple fire burning at night. It was only when actual signals were made that he could tell what they were intended for.

"It's some of the 'Paches, I s'pose. Lone Wolf is in trouble, but I don't know as we've got anything to do with it. The night is getting along, and we ought to be back to camp by this time."

Without waiting longer, he turned about and moved back into the wood, followed by his two friends.

It seemed strange to both of the latter that he could have left his mustang so far away from the place where his self-imposed duties had called him to bring to naught the cunning of his great enemy, the principal war-chief of the Apaches. But the truth was, the camps of the scout and the redskins were not so widely separated as Mickey and Fred believed. He had selected the best site possible, and took a roundabout course in going to or from it, as he had more means given him of concealing his trail. There were places where the soil was so rocky and stony that the foot left not the slightest imprint of its passage.

They had gone but a short distance from the ravine when they encountered one of the very stretches so valuable to persons in their predicament. No grass or vegetation of any kind impeded their way, and it was like walking over a hard, uncarpeted floor. Making their way across this, they struck into a wood that was denser than any they had encountered thus far. There their progress was slow, but they continued steadily forward, talking but little, and then in guarded tones. About the hour of midnight the camp of Sut Simpson was reached.

CHAPTER XXI

SAFETY AND SLEEP

There was nothing especially noticeable in the site which the scout had selected for his camp fire. His principal object had been secrecy and he had obtained it beyond all peradventure. The place was more like a cavern than anything else, except that it was open at the top, but it was walled in on the four sides, so there was barely room for the three to enter. As the scout explained, he was perfectly familiar with that section of the country, and he lost no time in hunting out the spot. He had his horse with him at the time the Apaches drove Mickey and Fred in among the rocks, and he staid until pretty certain they could keep the Apaches at bay until dark, when he made his way to a level spot inclosed by rocks. There he kindled a fire, cooked some antelope and left his mustang to graze and browse near by, while he returned to the assistance of his friends.

"Where did ye shoot that uncleope, or antelope?" asked Mickey.

"I didn't shoot him at all; he's the one you fetched down. Yer left enough for me, so I didn't run the risk of firing my gun when the varmints were so close by, so I sliced out a hunk or two from the carcass, and fetched it along."

"Ye haven't got any of it about ye?"

"Not enough for yer folks—no more than three or four pounds."

"Be the powers but ye're right. That's 'nough to stay our stomach, as me sick aunt remarked after swallowing her twenty-third dumpling."

At the moment the party walked in among the rocks the smoldering embers of the camp-fire were plainly seen. They needed but a little stirring to break forth into flame again, so as to light up the interior, which was about a dozen feet square, with a height of a dozen feet, more or less. When the Irishman signified that something in the way of food would be acceptable, the scout produced it from among the leaves near at hand, and it was devoured with the heartiest kind of appetite. They had drank all the water they needed, and the three assumed easy, lounging attitudes, Mickey lighting his pipe and enjoying himself immensely.

"This is what I call comfortable," he remarked, "as me friend Patsey McFadden observed when the row began at the fair and the whacks came from every quarter. I enjoy it; it's refining, it's soothing; it makes a man glad that he's alive."

"What do you think of it?" asked the scout, turning to Fred, who was reclining upon the heavy Apache blanket, with the appearance of one who was upon the verge of sleep.

"I feel very grateful to you," said he, rousing up, "and I am more contented than I have been in a long time; but I'm afraid all the time that Lone Wolf or some of his braves might find where we are."

Sut smiled in a pitying way, as he replied:

"Don't ye s'pose I'm old 'nough to fix all that? Haven't I larned 'nough of the 'Paches and thar devilments to keep 'em back? Wall, I rather guess I have."

As the night remained so warm that no comfort at all was derived from the fire, it was agreed that it should be left to burn out gradually. It had been kindled originally by Sut for the purpose of cooking his meat, and he had renewed it that his friends might see exactly where they were, and, at the same time, look into each other's faces.

"Let me ax ye," said Mickey, puffing away at his pipe, "whether, whin we start for home, we're going to take the pass, which seems as full of the spalpeens as me head is of grand ideas?"

"I can't be sartin of that," replied Sut, thoughtfully. "We can strike the prairie by going off here in another course; but it will take a long time, and the road is harder to travel. I like the pass a good deal the best, and unless the varmints seem too thick, we'll take it."

"If we could get a good, fair start in the pass, we could kape ahead of 'em all the way till we struck the open prairie, when it would be illigant to sail away and watch them falling behind, like a snail trying to catch a hare."

The scout pointed to the lad, and, turning his head, Mickey saw that he was sound asleep. The poor fellow was so wearied and worn that he could not resist the approach "tired nature's sweet restorer," which carried him off so speedily into the land of dreams.

"I'm glad to observe it," said the Irishman, "for the poor chap needs it. He's too young to be in this sort of business, but he couldn't prevint the soorcumstances, and we must help him out of the scrape as best we can."

"I'm with yer," responded the scout. "He's one of the most likely youngsters I've ever met, and I'll risk a good deal to fetch him along. I'm in hopes that we're purty well out of the woods, though we may have some trouble afore we get cl'ar of Lone Wolf and the rest."

"As soon as we get the critters to ride, I s'pose we kin be off."

"That's all, and that won't take me long. I'm used to finding horses that the varmints are fools 'nough to say are thars. One day last spring, I war over near the staked plain all alone, when I got cotched in one of them awful nor'easters, and I never came so near freezin' to death in all my life. Them sort of winds go right to the marrer of yer bones, and it takes yer a week to thaw out. Wall, sir, while I war tryin' to start a fire, a couple of Comanches managed to slip up and steal my mustang. I didn't find it out till three or four hours arter, and then I war mad. I couldn't stand no such loss, so I took the trail, and started off on a deer-trot arter 'em. Wall, sir, I chased them infernal varmints close on to twenty miles afore I run 'em to earth. Then I found 'em down into a deep holler, where I come nigh tumblin' heels over head right in atween 'em afore I knowed who they war. Yer see it war a piece of the meanest kind of business on thar part, 'cause they each had a mustang, and I hadn't any, and they war leadin' mine.

"I laid low for them varmints till night, when I mounted my critter, and struck off over the country leadin' thar two beasts with me. I expected they'd foller, of course, for the two animals that I captured were such beauties as you don't meet every day, so I kept 'em on the go purty steady for two days and nights, when I struck into the chapparal, tethered all three horses, tumbled over onto the ground, and put in four hours of straight solid sleep, such as makes a new man of a feller. Wall, sir, would you believe it? When I woke up and went to mount my hoss, he wasn't thar. Them same three skunks had managed to keep so close onto the trail, that, afore I woke, they slipped up, took all three of the animals, and were miles away when I opened my eyes.

"Wall, yer may skulp me if I wasn't mad, and I couldn't help laughin', too, to think how nice they had come it over me. As the game had begun atween us, I took the trail and follered it for half a week. Yer see, them skunks didn't mean that I shouldn't get the best of 'em agin. They rode fast, and kept it up as long as thar horses could stand it, by which time they had every reason to think they war a hundred miles ahead of me, and so they went in for a good rest, intending when they had got that to keep up thar flight till they reached thar village up near the headwaters of the Canadian. Of course thar wouldn't have been any show for me if I hadn't had a streak of luck. I know that country like a book, and I war purty sartin of the trail them thieves meant to take, so I started to cut across and head 'em off. I hadn't gone far when I come upon the camp of a Comanche war-party, numberin' a hundred. I hadn't any trouble in picking out an animal that suited, and then yer see I war all right, and, for fear I might get off the track, I come back and took up the trail again, and I kept it so hot that when they went into camp I warn't more than two miles away; I didn't want to come any closer, for if they'd found out that I war so near, they wouldn't have give me any kind of chance at all.

"I waited till it was dark, and thar wasn't a bit of moon that night, when I sneaked into camp and got thar three animals agin, and heading for Port Severn, I made up my mind to keep the thing going without giving 'em the slightest chance to pull up. The weather had toned down so that it was comfortable to travel, and arter I got out of hearin' of the camp, I just swung my hat, and kicked and laughed to think how cheap them varmints would feel when they'd come to wake up in the morning, and find out how nice the white man had got ahead of 'em. Yer see, it war just a question as to which of us war the smartest. We weren't going for each other's hair—though we'd done that any other time—but for each other's hosses, and I'd stole thars twice to thar stealin' mine once, and I still held 'em, so I had good reason to crow over 'em. Wal, sir, I made up my mind that they warn't going to come any shenanigan over me, and I struck the shortest line for Fort Severn. I rode through that very pass in which you come so near getting cotched, and in fact, the place whar I got the hosses warn't ten miles from that big cave.

"I had plain sailin' all the way into the fort, and everything went along well. I had only to ride on my critter, when the others galloped along like so many dogs. Yer see, I meant business, and I kept a watch for them varmints all the time. When I stopped for food or rest, I made sartin that they warn't anywhar in sight, and during the three or four days that followed I never slept an hour together. I managed to snatch a few minutes slumber while riding my mustang on a full gallop, but when I stopped to give the animals time to rest, I kept watch, for I felt as though it would break my heart to be outwitted again. I made the best kind of time, and my last camp was within a dozen miles of Fort Severn. I was purty well used up by that time, and making sure that the varmints warn't anywhar within a day's ride, I put in a good two hours sleep. Well I never rightly understood it," added Sut, with a sigh, "and I'm allers ashamed to tell it, but when I went out to mount my mustang, the whole four war gone, and the moccasin tracks on the ground showed who had took 'em. I can't understand to this day how them varmints kept so close behind me, and how they war ready when the chance came into their way; but they war, and they beat me as fairly as the thing was ever done in this world."

"Didn't ye try to folly them?"

"No; I thought I might as well give up. I sneaked into the fort and tried to keep the thing from 'em, but I couldn't tell a straight story, and they found out how it was at last, and I don't suppose I'll ever hear the last of it."

A short time afterward, the two laid down and slept.

CHAPTER XXII

TWO OLD ACQUAINTANCES

All three of the little party needed rest, and none of them opened their eyes until morning. As a simple precaution the scout smothered the fire entirely, by scraping the ashes over the embers. Not a ray of moonlight could reach them, and they were wrapped in the most impenetrable darkness.

As might be expected, Sut Simpson was the first to open his eyes, and by the time the sun was up all three were stirring. Enough meat remained over from the feast of the night before to furnish them with a substantial breakfast, and cool, refreshing water was at hand for drink and ablution. When the preliminaries had been completed, Sut went out to learn whether any of the Apaches were threateningly near. He wished, too, to prepare his horse for a ride to a point a dozen miles away, close to the margin of the prairie, where he intended to establish himself until he could procure the two animals that were needed by his companions. He had not been gone ten minutes when he came back in great excitement.

"My mustang is stole, or may I be skulped!" and then he added a general wail: "Them redskins are getting to be the greatest hoss-thieves in the world. I don't know what's to become of us if they're going to keep on in that way."

Mickey laughed heartily, for he recalled the narrative of the night before. In the game for horse flesh it looked very much as if the Apaches could be Sut's tutors.

"May I respectfully inquire where you got that crathur, in the first place?"

"Why, I bought him of the varmints."

"How mooch did you pay?"

"Wall," laughed Sut, in turn, "I haven't paid anything yet."

"I suppose they've sint in their account till they're tired. Finding yer doesn't pay any attention, they've come to take him back again."

"Are you sure that it was done by the Indians?" asked Fred, a little frightened at learning that they had been so close while he slept.

"Thar ain't a bit of doubt. I've looked the ground over, and thar's the trail, as plain as the nose on your face."

"How many?"

"Two."

"And they did it during the night?"

"No," replied the scout, displaying his wonderful woodcraft. "The varmints come yesterday arternoon, or just at dusk, arter I'd took supper and left."

"How do you know that?"

"I'd be a fool if I couldn't tell by the look of the trail how long ago it war made."

It seemed impossible that such was the fact, and yet, young as was Fred, he had heard of such things, and the scout spoke after the manner of one who meant what he said.

"Begorra, but it's meself that has it!" exclaimed Mickey, with a sudden lighting up of the countenance; "they're the same two spalpeens that took your hoss down by the Staked Plain, and then follyed ye up and did the same thing over again, just as ye was going into Fort Severn."

But the scout shook his head.

"The varmints don't know much about pity, but that's too rough a thing even for a Comanche to repeat. I've a s'picion that Lone Wolf had a hand in that, and I'm going for him. Come along."

And the indignant Sut strode out of camp, followed by his friends. He was not the man to submit to such a loss, and they saw that he was in deadly earnest. He neither spoke nor looked behind him for the next quarter of an hour, nor were his friends able to tell what direction he was following, for he changed so often, winding in and out among the trees, that they could form no conjecture as to the general course taken.

They saw that he was following a trail, for he continually looked down at the ground in front of him, and then glanced to the right and left, occasionally inclining his head, as though he was listening for something which he expected to hear. He appeared to be altogether unconscious of the fact that he had companions at all and they sought to imitate his stealthy, cat-like movement, without venturing to speak. After traveling the distance mentioned, and while they were moving along in the same cautious way, the scout suddenly wheeled on his knee, and faced them.

"See yer," said he; "it won't do for you to travel any further."

"What's up?" asked Mickey.

"Why, the trail's getting too hot. I ain't fur from them horses."

"Well, doesn't ye want us to stand by and obsarve the shtyle in which you are going to scoop them in?"

Simpson shook his head.

"Ye are both too green to try this kind of business. I never could get a chance at them varmints if I took yer along. All you've got to do is to stay yer till I get back. That won't be long."

"Suppose you don't get back at all?" asked Fred, anxiously.

"Then yer needn't wait."

"But ain't it probable that some of the Apaches will visit us?"

The scout was quite confident that the contingency would not occur; but, as long as they were in that part of the world, so long were they in danger of the redskins. It was never prudent to lay aside habits of caution; but he did not believe they were liable to molestation at that time. He charged them to keep quiet and always on the alert, and to expect his return within a couple of hours, although he might be delayed until noon. They were not to feel any apprehension unless the entire day should pass without his coming. Still, even that would be possible, he said, without implying anything more than that he had encountered unexpected difficulties in regaining his horse. They were still to wait for him until the morrow, and if he continued absent they were at liberty to conclude that the time had come for him to "pass in his checks." and they were to make the effort to reach home the best way they could. With this understanding they separated.

At the time Sut left his friends the trail was exceedingly "hot," as he expressed it, and he was confident that within the next half hour he could force matters to an issue. The scout was of the opinion that a couple of Apaches had accidently struck his trail, or happened directly upon his norse while he was grazing, and, without suspecting his ownership, aad taken him away. The trail led toward the Apache camp, although by a winding course, and that was not far away. He was desirous of coming up with the marauders before they joined in with the others. In that case he would consider himself fully equal to the task of getting even with them; but it was not likely that they would go into camp when they were so close to the main body.

Shortly after, to his great surprise, he came upon his mustang, tied by a long lariat to the limb of a tree, and contentedly grazing upon the grass, which was quite abundant. There was not the sign of an Indian visible.

"Skulp me! if that ain't a purty way to manage such things!" he exclaimed, astonished at the shape the matter had taken. "Them varmints couldn't have knowed that Sut Simpson owned that hoss, or they'd have tied him up tighter than that, and they'd had somebody down yer to watch him; but they war a couple of greenys, that's mighty sartin. It's a wonder they didn't fetch out some of thar mustangs, and leave 'em whar I could lay my hands onto 'em. But I rather think I've got my own hoss this time, as easy as a chap need expect to get anything in this world."

There was something so curious in the fact of the horse being left alone that Sut was a little suspicious, and decided to reconnoitre thoroughly before venturing further. He was partly hidden behind a large tree and had been so cautious and noiseless in his movements that his mustang, which was one of the quickest to detect the approach of any one, was unaware of his presence.

Sut was on the point of going forward, when a movement in the wood, on the other side of where the animal was grazing, attracted his attention, and he paused. At the same instant his steed lifted his head. There could be no doubt as to the cause, for within the next minute the figure of an Indian stepped forward toward the animal, and proceeded to examine him with a care and minuteness which showed that he expected to identify his ownership.

The eyes of Simpson lit up, and an expression of exultation crossed his countenance, not merely because the redskin before him was in his power, but because he recognized him as no one else but Lone Wolf, the Apache war-chief.

It looked as if the horse-thieves had approached the vicinity of camp with their plunder, and then, securing him to the branch of the tree, had gone in and reported what they had done. Lone Wolf, suspecting, perhaps, that it was the property of his enemy, Sut Simpson, had stolen out quietly and alone to satisfy himself. He knew all the "trade-marks" of the hunter so well that he could not be deceived. This was the theory which instantly occurred to Sut, who muttered to himself:

"Oh, it's *mine*, and I'm *here*, though you don't think it, and we'll soon shake hands over it!"

The scout speedily assured himself that Lone Wolf was

alone—that he had no half-dozen "retainers" who would immediately precipitate themselves upon him the instant a row should begin. Lone Wolf had no rifle with him, but carried his huge knife at his girdle—one of the most formidable instruments ever seen.

As he walked slowly about the mustang, scrutinizing him very carefully, he brought himself within a yard or two of where Sut Simpson crouched. The latter waited until he was the nearest, when he stepped forward, with his drawn knife in hand, and, placing himself directly in front of the astounded war-chief, said:

"*Now*, Lone Wolf, we'll make our accounts square!"

CHAPTER XXIII

BORDER CHIVALRY

As the scout uttered these words, the Apache whirled like lightning and drew his knife. His swarthy, painted face glowed with passion, and his black eyes twinkled with a deadly light. Seeing that he had no weapon but the knife, Sut Simpson, with a certain rude chivalry that did him credit, left his rifle leaning against the tree, while he advanced with a weapon corresponding to that of his enemy, so that both stood upon the same footing.

"Lone Wolf is glad to meet the white dog that he has hunted so long," said the chieftain, speaking English like a native.

With a sardonic grin Sut replied:

"That's played out, old Pockared"—alluding to the chieftain's pitted face. "I'm just as mad at yer as I kin be, without yer getting up any fancy didoes to upset my nerves. I've come for yer this time, and the best thing yer kin do is to proceed to business."

They were facing each other with drawn knives—almost toe to toe, and each waiting for the other to lead off. It would have been hard to tell which stood the best chance of winning.

Lone Wolf suddenly sprang forward like a panther, and made a vicious lunge with his knife, Sut easily avoiding it by leaping back, when, in turn, he made a similar attempt upon his adversary, who escaped in precisely the same manner. But the scout noticed an unaccountable thing. Lone Wolf had dropped his knife!

True, he picked it up like a flash, and put himself on guard, but how it was that a veteran like him could have made such a slip was totally inexplicable to his foe. But the explanation came the next moment, when the chief, without removing his eyes from those of the white man, cautiously changed the knife to his left hand. His right arm was injured in some way, so that it was unreliable. He had shown this, first by dropping the weapon while attempting to use it, and he showed it again by shifting it to his left hand, thus placing himself at a frightful disadvantage.

Sut saw no wound, yet there could be no doubt of the truth, and his feelings changed on the instant. He felt himself the meanest of men to attempt to overcome an almost helpless foe.

"Lone Wolf," said he, still looking him straight in the eyes, "why don't yer hold yer knife in the hand that yer generally do?"

"Lone Wolf can slay the dog of a white man with which hand he may choose."

"Yer haven't been able to do it with both hands during all these years that you've been tryin', when yer've had yer whole tribe to help yer; but don't make a fool of yerself, Lone Wolf. Are your right arm hurt?"

"Lone Wolf will fight the white dog with his strong arm."

"No, yer don't—that's played out," growled the scout, shoving his knife back in his girdle. "I don't love yer 'any more than I love the devil, and I felt happy to think that I had got a chance at last to git square with yer; but when I lift the top-knot of Lone Wolf and slide him under, he's got to have the same chance that I have. I don't believe you'd act that way toward me; but, then, you're a redskin, and that makes the difference. Lone Wolf, we'll adjourn the fight till you're yerself agin."

And, deliberately turning away, the scout vaulted upon the back of the mustang, cutting the lariat that held him by a sweep of the knife.

"I s'pose you'll own I've got some claim on this beast; so good-by."

And, without turning to look at him again, he rode deliberately away.

The Apache stood like a statute staring at him until he was hidden from view by the intervening trees. Then he turned and walked slowly in the opposite direction, no doubt with strange thoughts in his brain.

"I don't know how that scamp will take it," muttered Sut, as he rode along. "He's one of the ugliest dogs that ever wore a painted face; and if he could catch me with a broken arm or head, he wouldn't want anything better than to chop me up into mincemeat; but, as I told the old varmint himself, he's an Injin and I ain't, and that's what's the matter."

The wood was too dense and the ground too uneven to permit him to ride at a faster gait than a walk, but long before the appointed hour was up, he rejoined his friends, who were as surprised as pleased at his prompt reappearance.

"But where are the bastes that ye promised to furnish us?" inquired Mickey, who had very little relish for the prospect of walking any portion of the distance homeward.

"That's what I'll have for yer before the sun goes down," was the confident reply. "I'll get you one hoss, anyway, which, maybe, is just as good as two, for the weight of the younker don't make no difference, and we kin git along with one beast better than two."

"I submit to your suparior judgment," said the Irishman, deferentially, "and would suggist that the sooner the same quadruped is procured the better all round. I hope the thing won't be delayed, as me aunt obsarved when the joodge sintenced her husband to be hung."

Sut explained that his plan was to ride some distance further, to a spot which he had in mind, where they would be safer against being trailed. There, consequently, they could wait with more security while he went for the much-needed horse. Time was precious, and no one realized it more than Sut Simpson. He turned the head of his mustang toward the left, and, after he had started, leaped to the ground and walked ahead, acting the part of a guide for the horse as well as for his friends.

The surface over which they journeyed was of the roughest nature. The fact of it was, the scout was working the party out toward the open prairie, without availing himself of the pass—an undertaking which would have been almost impossible to any one else. At the same time, by picking his way over the rocky surface, and using all means possible to conceal their trail, he hoped to baffle any pursuit that might be attempted.

Lone Wolf was not the redskin to allow such a formidable

enemy as Sut Simpson to walk away unmolested, even though he had received an unexpected piece of magnanimity at his hands. He had learned that it was he who had played such havoc among his warriors the day before, who had deceived them by cunningly uttered signals, and had drawn away the redskins sufficiently to permit his two intended victims to walk out of his clutches. It had been a series of unparalleled exploits, the results of which would have exasperated the mildest tempered Indian ever known.

These thoughts were constantly in the mind of the scout as he picked out the path for his equine and human companions. He took unusual pains, for a great deal depended upon his success in hiding the trail as much as possible. Perhaps it is not correct to say that the Apaches could be thrown entirely off the scent, if they should set themselves to work to run the fugitives under cover. None knew this better than Sut himself, but he knew also that the thing could be partially done, and a partial success could be made a perfect one. That is, by adopting all the artifices at his command, the work of trailing could be rendered so difficult that it would be greatly delayed—so that it would require hours for the Apaches to unearth the hiding-place. And Sut meant to accomplish his self-imposed task during those few hours, so as to rejoin his friends, and resume their flight before the sharp-witted pursuers could overhaul them.

The journey, therefore, was made one of the most difficult imaginable. The mustang was unshod, and yet he clambered up steep places, and over rocks, and through gravelly gullies, where the ordinary horse would have been powerless. The animal seemed to enter into the spirit of the occasion and his performances again and again excited the wonder and admiration of Mickey and Fred. The creature had undergone the severest kind of training at the hands of an unsurpassed veteran of the frontier.

This laborious journeying continued for a couple of hours, during which it seemed to the man and lad that they passed over several miles of the roughest traveling they had ever witnessed. The mustang had fallen several times, but he sprang up again like a dog and showed no signs of injury or fatigue. Finally Sut made a halt, just as Mickey was on the point of protesting, and, turning about, so as to face his companions, he smiled in his peculiar way as he spoke.

"You've stood it pretty well for greenhorns, and now I'm going to give yer a good rest."

"Do you maan to go into camp for a week or a month, or until the warm season is over?"

"I'm going to leave yer here, while I go for some hoss flesh, and it'll take longer time than before."

But the Irishman insisted that he should be allowed to accompany the scout upon this dangerous expedition.

"For the raison that ye are going to pick out this animal for *me*," he added, "how do I know but what ye'll pick out some ring-boned, spavined critter that trots sideways, and is blind in both eyes?"

Fred, who dreaded the long spell of dreary waiting which seemed before him, asked that he might make one of the company; but Sut would not consent, and he objected to both. He finally compromised by agreeing to take the Irishman, but insisted that the lad should stay behind with his mustang.

"A younker like you couldn't do us a bit of good," added Sut, by way of explanation, "and like as not yer'd get us into the worst kind of difficulty. Better stay whar you be, rest and be ready to mount your new animal as soon as we're back, and scoot away for New Boston."

"How soon will you be back?" he asked, feeling that he ought to make no objection to the decision.

The forenoon was about half gone, and the scout looked up at the sky, removed his coon-skin cap, and thoughtfully wrinkled his brows, as though he were solving some important mental problem.

"Yer may skulp me, younker, but it's a mighty hard thing to tell. Now I got back with my own animile a good deal sooner than I expected, but that same thing ain't likely to happen agin. More likely it'll be t'other way, and we may be gone all day, and p'raps all night."

"And what am I to do all that time?"

"Wait; that'll be easy enough, arter such a rough tramp as I've given yer."

"But suppose some of the Indians come here; I haven't got any gun or pistol, so what shall I do?"

"The hoss thar will let you know when any of the varmints come sneaking round, and he'll do it, too, afore they know whar yer be, so you'll have time to dig out. I ain't much in the way of using a knife," added the scout. "I depends on me gun for a long range, and when I gets into close quarters, I throw this yer (tapping the handle of his knife), round careless like; but I've got a little plaything yer that has stood me well, once or twice, and if it's any help to yer, why, yer are welcome to it. It was give to me by an officer down at Fort Massachusetts."

As he spoke, the scout drew a small revolver, beautifully mounted and ornamented with silver, which he handed to the lad, who, as may be supposed, was delighted with the weapon.

"Just the thing, exactly," he said, as he turned it over in his hand. "There are five barrels."

"And every one is loaded," added the scout. "The pill which it gives a redskin ain't very big, but it's sure, and it'll hunt for him a good ways off; so the dog is apt to bite better than you expect."

Sut told him that he expected to return by nightfall, and possible before, but they might be kept away until morning. Under any circumstances, whether successful or not, they would be back within twenty-four hours, for they could better afford to wait and repeat the attempt than to stay away longer than that. The reason for this decision was that if any of the Apaches should attempt to trail them, and there was every reason to believe that they would, they would not need more than twenty-four hours to track them to this hiding place. It was especially necessary that a collision with them should be avoided as long as possible, for the whites had everything to gain by such a course. As time was valuable, Sut did not delay the departure, and, as he and Mickey gave the lad a cheery good-by, they turned off to the right, and a minute later disappeared from view.

"Here I am alone again," he said to himself, "excepting the horse, and I've got a loaded revolver. Sut don't think those Apaches can get here before to-morrow morning, and he knows more than I do about it, so I hope he's right. We've got thus far on our way home, and it would be a pity if we should fail."

As he looked around, he saw nothing in the place or surroundings which would have commended it to him. There was water in the shape of a trickling stream, and that was plenty everywhere, but there was scarcely a spear of grass visible. The vegetation was stunted and unthrifty in appearance. There were stones and rocks everywhere, with nothing that could serve as a shelter in case of storm. He searched for a considerable distance around, but was unable to find even a shelving rock, beneath which he might creep and gather himself up if one of those terrific tempests peculiar to this region should happen to strike him. Nor did there seem to be any suitable refuge if the Apaches should attack him before he could retreat.

He might crouch down behind some of the boulders and rocks, but the make-up of the surface around him was so similar that three red skins could surround him with perfect ease and without any danger to themselves. Fred therefore made up his mind that he was in about as uncomfortable a situation as a fugitive could well be.

CHAPTER XXIV

NIGHT VISITORS

As young Munson expected to remain where he was for the rest of the day, and perhaps through the succeeding night, and knew that he was in great danger, he made it his business to acquaint himself thoroughly with his position and with all the approaches thereto. The first natural supposition was that the Apaches, in following the fugitives to the spot, would, from the force of circumstances, keep to the trail, that being their only guide.

This trail, for the last two hundred yards, led up a slope to where he was stationed upon what might have been called a landing in the ascent of the mountain. At the bottom of this two hundred yards or so was an irregular plateau, beyond which the trail was lost.

"If the Apaches should show themselves before dark," he concluded, as he looked over the ground, "there is where they will be seen, and that's the spot I must watch so long as I can see it."

Fred was able to hide himself from view for the time being, but there was no way in which he could conceal the horse. He was sure to be the first object that would attract the eye of

Lieut. R. H. Jayne

the redskins from below, revealing to them the precise position of the fugitives. This reflection disturbed the lad a good deal, until he succeeded in convincing himself that, after all, it was fortunate that it was so.

The redskins, detecting the mustang among the rocks, would believe that the three whites were there on the defensive. No matter if their force were a half dozen times as great, they would make the attack with a great deal of caution, and would probably manoeuvre around until dark, in the expectation of a desperate fight—all of which Fred hoped would give him a good chance of stealing out and escaping them.

This, as a matter of course, was based upon the idea that Sut Simpson, the veteran scout, had committed a serious error in believing that the pursuit would be slow. And such a mistake he had indeed made, as the lad discovered in due time.

The afternoon wore slowly away, and sunset was close at hand, when Fred was lying upon his face, peering over the upper edge of a rock at the plateau below. The fact of it was, his eyes had been roaming over the same place so long, that the stare had become a dreary, aimless one. He was suddenly aroused, however, to the most intense attention by the discovery of an Apache warrior, who drifted very serenely into the field of vision as if he were part of a moving panorama upon which the lad was gazing.

The boy had been waiting so long for his appearance that he uttered an exclamation, and half arose to his feet in his excitement. But he quickly settled back again, and, with an interest which it would be hard to describe, watched every movement of the redskin, as the tiger watches the approach of its victim.

The indian stalked up the other side of the plateau, walking slowly, looking right and left, in front and rear, and down at the ground, his manner showing that he was engaged in trailing the party, using all the care and skill of which he was the master. Reaching the middle of the plateau, he stopped, looked about, and made a gesture to some one behind him. A moment later, a second indian appeared, and then a third, the trio meeting near the centre of the irregular plot, where they immediately began a conversation.

Each of the three was liberal with his gestures, and now and then Fred could catch the sound of their voices. What it was that could so deeply interest them at such a time, he was at a loss to conjecture, but there could be no doubt that it related to the party they were pursuing.

"That must be all there are of them," he reflected, after several minutes had passed, without any other Apaches becoming visible; "but it seems to me it is a small force to chase us with. I've always understood that the Indians wanted double the number of their enemies, whenever they are going to attack them, but I suppose they've got some plan that I can't understand."

They had been talking but a short time, when Fred understood from their actions that they had detected the mustang above them on the mountain side. They looked up several times, and pointed and gesticulated in the same earnest fashion. It suddenly occurred to the lad that he might play a good point on the redskins, with the idea of delaying any offensive movement they might have under discussion. Pointing his revolver over the rock in front of him, he pulled the trigger.

The report was as sharp and loud almost as that of a rifle, but the parties against whom it it was aimed were in no more danger than if they had been in the city of Newark. The report had no sooner reached the ears of the Apaches than they scattered as wildly as if they had heard the whizz of a dozen bullets by their faces. Fred chuckled over the success of his ruse and made sure to keep himself hid from view.

"That will make them think that we're holding a sharp look-out for them, and they'll be careful before they make an attack upon us."

It seemed strange to him that the Apaches, who must know of the presence of Sut Simpson, who was equal to half a dozen men in such a situation, should have sent forward only three of their warriors to trail him.

"It may be," he thought, after a while, "that these men know how to follow a trail faster than the others, and they have gone on ahead, while the others are coming after them. I should think Lone Wolf would do anything in the world to catch Sut, who has done him so much injury."

Night was drawing on apace, darkness being due in less than an hour. Fred was naturally perplexed and alarmed, for he could not help feeling that he was in a most perilous position, regarding which he should have had more advice from the scout before his departure. The only thing that seemed prudent for him to do was to wait until dark and then quietly steel out and shift his position. It looked very much as if he could take care of himself for the night, at least, but he did not see how he could take care of the mustang, which had already changed hands so often, and which was so necessary to their safety.

"Sut said he expected to be home by dark, and I wish he'd come," was the thought that passed through his mind over and over again as he looked into the gathering darkness and listened for the sound of his friends.

But the stillness remained unbroken and the shadows deepened, until he saw that the night was fully come, and he could move about without danger of being fired upon from a distance. The moon was late in rising, so that the gloom was deep enough to hide one person from another, when the distance was extremely slight. Although aware of this, Fred was afraid of some flank movement upon the part of the Apaches, before he could get out of their reach. The suspicion that there were two men besides would make the redskins very cautious in their movements, but a little manoeuvring on their part might reveal the truth, in which case the situation of the lad would be critical in the extreme.

Fred had nerved himself to the task of stealing around the corner of a large rock and off into the darkness, when he was startled by a quick, sudden stamp of the horse. There might have been nothing in this; but, recalling what the scout had said about the skill of the animal as a sentinel, he had no doubt but that it meant that he had scented danger and that the redskins were close at hand. Scarcely pausing to reflect upon the advisability of the step, the lad began crawling in the direction of the animal, not more then twenty feet away.

Before he had passed half the distance he was certain that a redskin was at some deviltry, for the horse stamped and snorted, and showed such excitement, that Fred forgot his own danger, and, springing to his feet, ran rapidly toward the animal. Just as he reached him, he saw that an Indian had him by the bridle, and was trying to draw him along, the mustang resisting, but still yielding a step at a time. In a short time, if the thief was not disturbed, he would have gotten him beyond the possibility of rescue, he seeming more anxious to secure the steed than the scalp of its owner. With never a thought of the consequences, Fred raised his

Lieut. R. H. Jayne

revolver and blazed away with both barrels, aiming as best he could straight at the marauding Apache, who, with a howl of rage and terror, dropped the bridle of the mustang and bounded away among the rocks.

"There! I guess when you want to borrow a horse again, you'll ask the owner."

The lad was reminded of his imprudence by the flash of a rifle almost in his face, and the whizz of the bullet which grazed his cheek. But he still had two loaded chambers in his revolver, and he wheeled for the purpose of sending one of them at least, into the warrior that had made an attempt upon his life. At this critical juncture the mustang displayed an intelligence that was wonderful.

The Apache who was stealing upon him was near the steed, which, without any preliminary warning, let out both his heels, knocking the unsuspecting wretch fully a dozen feet and stretching him, badly wounded, upon the ground.

"I wonder how many more there are?" exclaimed the lad, looking about him, and expecting to see others rushing forward from the gloom.

But the repulse for the time being was effectual and the way was clear.

"I guess I'd better get out of here," was the thought of Fred, "for it ain't likely they will leave me alone very long when they've found out that I'm the only one left."

With revolver in hand he moved hurriedly backward among the rocks, and, after going a few rods, halted and looked for his pursuers, whom he believed to be close behind him. There was something coming, but a moment's listening satisfied him that it was his mustang, which seemed to comprehend the exigency fully as well as he did himself.

"I don't know about that," he reflected. "They can follow him better then they can me, and he can't sneak along like I can. If they catch him, they'll be pretty sure to catch me."

He started to flee, not from the Indians only, but from the mustang as well. But the speed of the latter was greater than his own, and, after several attempts to dodge him, he gave it up.

"If you can travel so well," reflected Fred, "you might as well carry me on your back."

Saying this he leaped upon the animal's back and gave him free rein. The animal was going it on his own hook and he plunged and labored along for some minutes longer, over the rockiest sort of surface, until he halted of his own accord. The instant he did so Fred leaped to the ground, paused and listened for his pursuers. Nothing but the hurried breathing of the mustang could be heard. The latter held his head well up, with ears thrown forward, in the attitude of attention. But minute after minute passed and the stillness remained unbroken. It looked indeed as if the fugitive horse and boy had found rest for the time, and, so long as the darkness continued, there was no necessity for further flight.

CHAPTER XXV

HUNTING A STEED

Leaving Fred Munson to watch for the approach of the Indians, it becomes necessary to follow Mickey O'Rooney and Sut Simpson on their hunt for a horse with which to continue their flight from the mountains and across the prairies. It cannot be said that the scout, in starting upon this expedition, had any particular plan in view. As he remarked, Indians were around them, and, wherever Indians were found, it was safe to look for the best kind of horses. Wherever the best opportunity offered, there he intended to strike. With this view, the first position of their expedition was in the nature of a survey, by which they intended to locate the field in which to operate.

The Irishman could not fail to see the necessity of caution and silence, and, leaving his more experienced companion to take the lead, he followed him closely, without speaking or halting. The way continued rough and broken, being very difficult to travel at times; but after they had tramped a considerable distance, Mickey noticed that they were going down hill at quite a rapid rate, and finally they reached the lowermost level, where the scout faced him.

"Do yer know whar yer be?" he asked, in a significant tone.

"Know whar I be?" repeated the Irishman, in amazement. "How should I know, as the spalpeens always said arter I knocked them down at the fair? What means of information have I?"

"You've been over this spot afore," continued the scout, enjoying the perplexity of his friend.

The latter scratched his head and looked about him with a more puzzled expression than ever.

"The only place that it risimbles in my mind, is a hilly portion in the north of Ireland. Do you maan to say we've arrived thar?"

"This is the pass which you tramped up and down, and whar you got into trouble."

"It don't look like any part that I ever obsarved; but why do you have such a hankering for this ravine, in which we haven't been used very well?"

"Yer's whar the Injuns be, and yer's whar we must look for hosses—sh!"

Mickey heard not the slightest sound, but he imitated the action of the scout and dodged down in some undergrowth, which was dense enough to hide them from the view of any one who did not fairly trample upon them. They had crouched but a minute or two in this position, when Mickey fancied he heard the tramp of a single horse, approaching on a slow walk. He dared not raise his head to look, although he noticed that the shoulders of the scout in front of him were slowly rising, as he peered stealthily forward.

The experiences of the last few days had been remarkable in

more than one respect. The two men had set out to secure a horse, neither deeming it probable that the one which was desired above all others could be obtained; and yet, while they were crouching in the bushes, the very animal—the one which had been ridden by Mickey O'Rooney—walked slowly forth to view, on his way up the ravine or pass. The most noticeable feature of the scene was that he was bestrode by an Indian warrior, whose head was bent in a meditative mood. The redskin, so far as could be seen, was without a companion, the steed walking at the slowest possible gait and approaching a point which was no more than a dozen feet away.

The instant Mickey caught sight of the warrior and recognized his own horse, there was a slight movement on the part of the scout. The Irishman narrowly escaped uttering an exclamation of surprise and delight as he identified his property, but he checked himself in time to notice that Sut was stealthily bringing his gun around to the front, with the unmistakable purpose of shooting the Apache. The heart of the Irishman revolted at such a proceeding. There seemed something so cowardly in thus killing an adversary without giving him an opportunity to defend himself that he could not consent to it. Reaching forward, he twitched the sleeve of Sut, who turned his head in surprise.

"What is it ye're driving at, me laddy?"

"Sh!—him!" he whispered, in return, darting his head toward the slowly approaching horseman, winking and blinking so significantly that it was easy to supply the words which were omitted.

"But why don't ye go out and tell him what ye intend, so that he can inform his friends, and bid them all good-bye? It ain't the thing to pop a man over in that style, without giving him a chance to meditate on the chances of his life, so be aisy wid him, Soot."

The scout seemed at a loss to understand the meaning of his companion, whose waggery and drollery cropped out at such unexpected times that no one knew when to expect it. The Indian was approaching and was already close at hand. Keen-eared, and with their senses always about them, Apaches are likely to detect the slightest disturbance. The scout glanced at the horseman, and then at Mickey, who was in earnest.

"It's the only way to git the hoss, you lunkhead, so will yer keep yer meat-trap shet?"

"I don't want a horse if we've got to murder a man to git the same."

"But the only way out here to treat an Injin is to shoot him the minute yer see him—that's sensible."

"I don't want ye to do it," said Mickey, so pleadingly that the scout could not refuse.

"Wal, keep still and don't interfere, and I promise yer I won't slide him under, onless he gits in the way, and won't git out."

"All right," responded Mickey, not exactly sure that he understood him, but willing to trust one who was not without his rude traits of manhood.

All this took place in a few seconds, during which the Apache horseman had approached, and another moment's delay would have given him a good chance of escape by flight. As noiselessly as a shadow the scout arose from his knees to a stooping position, took a couple of long, silent strides forward, and then straightened up, directly in front of the startled horse, and still more startled rider. The former snorted, and partly reared up, but seemed to understand, as if by an instinct, that the stranger was more entitled to claim him than the one upon his back. Another step forward and the scout held the bridle in his left hand, while he addressed the astounded Apache in his own tongue, a liberal translation being as follows:

"Let my brother, the dog of an Apache, slide off that animile, and vamoose the ranch, or I'll lift his ha'r quicker'n lightning."

The savage deemed it advisable to "slide." He carried a knife at his girdle, and held a rifle in his grasp, but the scout had come upon him so suddenly that he felt he was master of the situation. So without attempting to argue the matter with him, he dropped to the ground, and began retreating up the ravine, with his face toward his conquerer, as if he mistrusted treachery.

"Our blessing go wid ye," said Mickey, rising to his feet, and waving his hand toward the alarmed Apache; "we don't want to harm ye, and ye may go in pace. There, Soot," he added, as he came up beside him, "we showed that spalpeen marcy whin he scarcely had the right to expict it, and he will appreciate the same."

"Ye're right," grunted the scout. "He'll show ye how he'll appreciate it the minute he gets a chance to draw bead onto yer; but ye've larned that thar are plenty of varmints in this section, and if we're going to get away with this hoss thar ain't no time to lose. Up with yer thar and take the bridle."

Mickey did as he requested, not exactly understanding what the intention was.

"What is to be done?" he asked, as the head of the animal was turned back over the route that he had just traveled. "Am I to ride alone, while ye walk beside me?"

"That's the idea for the present, so as to save the strength of the horse. A half mile or so up the pass is a trail which leads down inter it. The mustang can go over that like a streak of greased lightning, and thar's whar we'll leave the pass, and make off through the woods and mountains, till we can jine in with the younker and go it without trouble."

A few words of hurried consultation completed the plans. As they were very likely to encounter danger, it was agreed that the scout should go ahead of the horseman, keeping some distance in advance, and carefully reconnoitering the way before him with a view of detecting anything amiss in time to notify his friend, and prevent his running into it. There might come a chance where it would not be prudent for Sut Simpson to press forward, but where, if the intervening distance was short, Mickey might be able to make a dash for the opening in the pass and escape with his mustang. The Apache, being unhorsed in the manner described, had fled in the opposite direction from that which they intended to follow. Of course he could get around in front, and signal those who were there of what was coming, provided the two whites were tardy in their movements, which they didn't propose to be.

It required only a few minutes to effect a perfect understanding, when the scout went a hundred yards or so ahead, moving forward at an ordinary walk, scanning the ravine right, left and in front, and on the watch for the first sign of danger. He had previously so located and described the opening by which they expected to leave the pass, that Mickey was sure he would recognize it the instant they came in sight of it. This was a rather curious method of procedure, but it was continued for a time, and the avenue alluded to was nearly in sight when Sut Simpson, who was a little further than usual in advance, suddenly stopped and raised his hand as a signal for his friend to stop.

Mickey did so at once, holding the mustang in check, while he watched the scout with the vigilance of a cat. Sut never once looked behind him, but his long form gradually sank down in the grass, until little more than his broad shoulders and a coon-skin cap were visible. The pass at that place was anything but straight, so that the view of Mickey was much less than that of the scout; and, had it been otherwise, it is not likely that the former would have been able to read the signs which were as legible to the latter as the printed pages of a book.

"Begorrah, but that's onplisant!" muttered the Irishman to himself, "We must be moighty close onto the door, when some of the spalpeens stick up their heads and object to our going out. Be the powers! but they may object, for all I care. I'm going to make a run for it!"

At this juncture the figure of the scout was seen approaching in the same guarded manner.

"Well, Soot, me laddy, what do ye make of it?"

"Thar's a party of the varmints just beyont the place we meant to ride out."

"Well, what of that? You can lave the pass somewhere along here, where there seem plenty of places that ye can climb out, while I make a dash out of that, and we'll meet agin after we get clear of the spalpeens."

"Thar's a mighty risk about it, and yer be likelier to get shot than to be missed."

"That's all right," responded Mickey. "I'm reddy to take the chances in that kind of business. Lead on, and we'll try it. It'll soon be dark, and I'm getting tired of this fooling."

Sut liked that kind of talk. There was a business ring about it, and he responded:

"I'll go ahead, and when it's time to stop I'll make yer the signal. Keep watch of my motions."

Ten minutes later they had reached a spot so near the opening that Mickey easily recognized it. He compressed his lips and his eyes flashed with a stern determination as he surveyed it. The scout was still in the advance, proceeding in the same careful manner, all his wits about him, when he again paused, and motioned for the Irishman to stop. The latter saw and recognized the gesture, but he declined to obey it. He permitted his mustang to walk on until he had reached the spot where Sut was crouching, making the most furious kind of motions, and telling him to stay where he was.

"Why didn't yer stop when I tell yer, blast ye?" he demanded angrily.

"Is that the place where ye expected to go out?" asked Mickey, without noticing the question, as he pointed off to the spot which he had fixed upon as the one for which they were searching.

"Of course it is; but what of it? You can't do anything thar."

"I'll show ye, me laddy; I'm going there as sure as me name's Mickey O'Rooney, and me."

"Yer ain't going to try any such thing; if yer do, I'll bore yer."

But the Irishman had already given the word to his horse. The latter bounded forward, passing by the dumbfounded hunter, who raised his rifle, angered enough to tumble the reckless fellow from the saddle. But, of course, he could not do that, and he stared in a sort of a wondering amazement at the course of the Irishman. The latter, instead of seeking to conceal his identity, seemed to take every means to make it known. He put the mustang on a dead run, sat bolt upright on his back, and Sut even fancied that he could see that his cap was set a little to one side, so as to give himself a saucy, defiant air to whomsoever might look upon him.

"Skulp me! if he ain't a good rider!" exclaimed the scout, anxious to assist him in the trouble with which he was certain to environ himself. "But he is riding to his death. Thar! what next? He's crazy."

This exclamation was caused by seeing Mickey lift his cap and swing it about his head, emitting at the same time a number of yells such as no Apache among them all could have surpassed.

"Whoop! whoop! ye bloody spalpeens! it's meself, Mickey O'Rooney, that's on the war-path, and do ye kape out of the way, or there'll be some heads broken."

Could madness further go? Instead of trying to avoid an encounter with the Apaches, the belligerent Irishman seemed actually to be seeking it. And there was no danger of his being disappointed. Certain of this, Sut Simpson hurried on after him, for the purpose of giving what assistance he could in the desperate encounter soon to take place.

Mickey was still yelling in his defiant way, with the long,

lank figure of the scout trotting along in the rear, when one, two, three, fully a half dozen Apaches sprang from the ground ahead of the Irishman, and, as if they divined his purpose, all began converging toward the opening which was the goal of the fugitive. But it would have made no difference to the latter if a score had appeared across his path. He hammered the ribs of his mustang with his heels, urging him to the highest possible speed of which he was capable. Then he replaced his cap, added an extra yell or two, raised his rifle and sighted best as he could at the nearest Indian. When he pulled the trigger, he missed the mark probably twenty feet, for it was a kind of business to which Mickey was unaccustomed.

The Apaches threw themselves across his path, in the hope of checking the mustang so as to secure the capture of the rider; but the animal abated not a tittle, and strained every nerve to carry his owner through the terrible gauntlet. One of the redskins, fearful that the fugitive was going to escape in spite of all they could do, raised his gun, with the purpose of tumbling him to the ground. Before he could do anything, he dropped his gun, threw up his arms with a howl, and tumbled over backward. Sut Simpson was near enough at hand to send in the shot that wound up his career.

By this time, something like a sober second thought came to Mickey, who saw that his horse comprehended what was expected of him, and needing do further direction or urging. He realized, furthermore, that he had, by the impetuous movement of the animal, thrown all his foes in the rear, and they being unmounted, and anxious to check his flight, were certain to give him the contents of their rifles. Accordingly he threw himself forward upon the neck of the steed, scarcely a second before the crack of the rifles were heard in every direction. The hurtling bullets passed fearfully near, and more than once Mickey believed he was struck. But his horse kept on with unabated speed, and a minute after thundered up the slope, and he and his rider were beyond the reach of all their bullets.

CHAPTER XXVI

LONE WOLF'S TACTICS

Mickey O'Rooney gave a yell of defiance as he vanished from view, horse and rider unharmed by the scattering shots which followed them, even after they were lost to sight. It was well and bravely done, and yet it would have failed altogether but for the wonderful cunning and shrewd courage of Simpson, who had kept close to the heels of the flying horse. It was when the crisis came—when the Apaches were closing around the fugitive, and it seemed inevitable that he should reap the natural reward of his own foolhardiness that Sut had acted. When the warriors were confident of their success, he discharged his rifle with marvelous quickness, and with a more important result than the mere tumbling over of his man.

There was a momentary check, a sudden stoppage, lasting but a few seconds, when the foe rallied and made for the fugitive. But that brief interval of time was precisely what was needed, and it secured the safety of Mickey and his steed. It mattered not that Sut Simpson as good as threw away his life by his chivalrous act. He knew that full well, while awaiting the opportunity, as much as he did when he raised his faithful weapon and discharged it into the group.

Lieut. R. H. Jayne

The moment the piece was fired he knew that his mission was accomplished, and he began a retreat, moving stealthily and rapidly backward, for the purpose of getting beyond the range of the redskins before they should fairly recover from the escape of the horseman. But events were proceeding rather too rapidly. Before he could cover any appreciable distance, the baffled wretches turned upon him and it was flight or fight, or, more likely, both.

The Apaches were brave, they knew the character of the dreaded scout and they were not desirous of rushing, one after another, to their doom. Sut was certain that, if he should turn and run, the howling horde would be at his heels. The instant there should appear any possibility of his escape, they would all open upon him, and it was impossible that any such good fortune should attend him as had marked the flight of Mickey. It was his purpose, therefore, to keep up his retreat with his face to his foe, forcing all to maintain their distance, until he could reach the side of the ravine, where, possibly, a sudden desperate effort might enable him to outwit the redskins.

The scout had not yet been given time in which to reload his piece, but the uncertainty whether it contained another charge prevented them from making an impetuous rush upon him. Besides, they knew that he carried a formidable knife, and, like every border character, he was a professor of the art of using it. All at once it occurred to Sut that he might thin out his assailants by the use of his revolver. If he could drop three or four, or more, and then follow it up with a savage onslaught, he believed he could open the way. He felt for the weapon, and was terribly disappointed to find it gone.

He recalled that he had given it to Fred Munson when he was left alone with the mustang. So, as he had nothing but his knife, he placed his hand upon the haft, glaring defiantly at his enemies, while he continued walking slowly backward, and gradually edging toward the side of the grove. But Apaches were plenty in that latitude, and the business had scarcely opened when three or four warriors commenced a stealthy approach upon the scout from the rear. He glanced hastily over his shoulder several times, while slowly retreating, to guard against this very danger; but the Indians, seeing the point for which the fugitive was making, ensconced themselves near it and waited.

At the moment Sut placed his hand upon the knife, he was within twenty feet of the three Indians crouching in the grass, with no suspicion of their proximity. One of them arose to his feet, quietly swung a coiled lasso about his head (the distance being so slight that no great effort was necessary), and then with great dexterity dropped it over the head of the unsuspicious scout, inclosing his arms, when he jerked it taut with the suddenness of lightning.

A few seconds only were necessary for Sut to free himself, but ere those seconds could be taken advantage of, he was drawn over backward. The entire party sprang upon him and seized his gun and knife.

"Skulp me, if this don't look as though I'd made a slip of it this time!" muttered Sut, as he bounded like lightning to his feet. "When yer varmints undertake a job of this kind, yer show that yer ain't no slouches, but have a good knowledge of the business."

As if anxious to deserve the complimentary opinion of their distinguished prisoner, they coiled the lasso again and again about him, until he was fastened by a dozen rounds and was no more able to contend against his captors then if he were an infant.

Lieut. R. H. Jayne

As all the warriors recognized the prisoner, their delight was something extraordinary. They danced about him in the most grotesque and frantic manner, screeching, yelling, and indulging in all sorts of tantalizing gestures and signs at Simpson, who was unable to resist them or help himself.

There was a certain dignity in the carriage of Sut under these trying circumstances. Instead of replying by taunts to the taunts of his enemies, he maintained silence, permitting them to wag on to their heart's content.

It was wonderful how rapidly the tidings of the capture spread. The hootings and yellings that marked the rejoicings of the party were heard by those who were further away, and they signaled it to the warriors beyond. The redskins came from every direction, and, within half an hour from the time Sut Simpson was lassoed, there must have been nearly a hundred Apaches gathered around him. These all continued their frantic rejoicings, while, as before, the prisoner remained silent.

His eyes were wandering over the company in search of Lone Wolf, their great leader; but that redoubtable chieftain was nowhere to be seen. Sut was certain that he was somewhere near at hand, and must know of all that had happened on this spot.

Did Simpson expect anything like mercy from the Apaches? Not a whit of it. He had fought them too long, had inflicted too much injury, and understood them too thoroughly to look for anything of the kind. Besides, even if he was innocent of having ever harmed a redskin, he would not have received the slightest indulgence at their hands. The Apaches are like all the rest of their species, in their inherent opposition to mercy on general principles.

The afternoon was well spent, and, as a means of occupying his mind until his case was disposed of, he set himself speculating as to what their precise intentions were. Being quite familiar with the Apache tongue, he caught the meaning of many of their expressions; but for a considerable time these were confined to mere exultations over his capture. The excitement was too great for anything like deliberation, or concerted council.

"It may be the skunks are waitin' fur Lone Wolf," he muttered, as he stood with his arms bound to his side. "They wouldn't dare to do much without axing him, though I 'spose they might a skulp any man wherever they got the chance, without stopping to ax questions. Helloa! thar he comes!"

This exclamation was caused by the sudden turning of heads, and a sort of hush that fell upon the group for the moment, close to the approach of someone on horseback. It was already so close to dusk that he could not be identified until he came closer, when Sut was surprised to find that it was not the chieftain, after all. It was a man altogether different in appearance, probably a subordinate chief, who had performed some daring deed which had won him the admiration of his comrades. The indications, too, were that he brought interesting news about something.

"That varmint has been away somewhar," concluded Sut, carefully noting everything, "and they expect him to tell something worth hearin', and I guess they're about kerrect, so I'll see what I kin do in the way of listening myself."

The scout was right in his supposition. The Indian was the *avant courier* of a party three or four times as great as that which had gathered about him in the ravine. His companions had separated and gone in other directions, while he, learning the course taken by his chief, Lone Wolf, had hastened to report directly to him.

Sut Simpson suspected what all this meant. He saw a number of scalps hanging at the girdle of the Apache, and he had not listened long when his fears where more than confirmed. The embryo town of New Boston, planted in the valley of the Rio Pecos, was no more. Repulsed bloodily at the first, Lone Wolf had gathered together the best of his warriors, placed them under one of his youngest and most daring chiefs, and sent them forth with orders to clean out the settlement that had been planted so defiantly in the heart of their country. And now this chief had returned to say that the work had been completed, precisely as commanded.

"I knowed it war coming," muttered the scout. "I told that Barnwell that Lone Wolf would bounce him afore he knowed what the the matter was, and I urged 'em to make for Fort Severn, which war only fifty miles away, and save their top-knots. He did not say so, but I could see he thought I war a big fool, and now he's found out who the fool was. Wonder whether any of the poor cusses got away? Thar couldn't have been much chance. 'Twon't do to ax this rooster, cause he wouldn't be likely to answer me, and, if he did, he would be sartin' to tell me a lot of lies."

The young chief having communicated his good tidings, and exchanged congratulations with those about him, started his mustang forward, heading him directly up the ravine or pass. This brought him within arm's length of the scout, who was standing mute and motionless. The redskin drew up his horse and stared fixedly at him, as if, for the moment, uncertain of his identity.

"I'm Sut Simpson, the man that has slain so many Apache warriors that he cannot number them," said the scout, with a view of helping the Indian to recognize him.

There was no real braggadocio about this. As Sut could not hide his personality, the best plan for him was to make an open avowal, backed up by a rather high-sounding vaunt. This was more pleasing to the Indians, who were addicted to the most extravagant kind of expression.

Rather curiously, the young chief made no reply. The observation of the prisoner seemed to have settled all doubts that were in his mind, and perhaps he was desirous of seeing Lone Wolf without any further delay. His steed struck into a rapid gallop, and speedily vanished in the gloom, leaving the captive with the howling hundred.

Sut was brave, but there was a certain feeling of disappointment that began to make itself felt. Although he would not have admitted it, yet the termination of the recent meeting with Lone Wolf, had led him to hope, not that the chieftain would liberate him, but that he would give him some kind of a show for his life—an opportunity, no matter how desperate, in which he might make a fight for his existence. He had spared Lone Wolf when he was at his mercy, refusing to fight the chief because he was so disabled that his defeat was assured. It would seem that the chief, in return, might offer the scout a chance to fight some of the best warriors; and such probably would have been the case with any set of people except the American Indians. The absence of Lone Wolf impressed Sut very unfavorably. He believed the chief meant to remain away until after his important prisoner was killed.

By the time night was descended, the wild rejoicing in a great measure ceased. One of the Apaches started a fire, and the others lent their assistance. A roaring, crackling flame lit up a large area of the ravine, revealing the figure of every savage, as well as that of the scout, who, having grown weary of continual standing, seated himself upon the ground.

Had Sut possessed the use of his arms, he would have made an effort to get away at this time. A short run would have carried him to the place which he had in mind at the time he began his retreat. Without the aid of his hands, however, he was certain to be entrapped again, so he concluded to remain where he was, with the hope that something more inviting would present itself.

The frontiersman never despairs; and, although it was difficult to figure out the basis of much hope in the present case, yet Sut held on, and determined to do so to the end. He made several cautious tests of his bonds, but the lariat of buffalo-hide was wound around his arms so continuously, and tied so well, that the strength of twenty men could not have broken it. The exploit of cutting them by abrasion against a sharp stone (which he had once done), could not be accomplished in the present instance, for the reason that there was no suitable stone at hand, and he was under too strict surveillance. And so it only remained for him to wait and hope, and hold himself in readiness.

When the fire had crackled and flamed for a while, the Apaches clustered in groups upon the ground, where they smoked and talked incessantly. They seemed to be paying no attention to their prisoner, and yet they took pains to group themselves around him in such a way that if he should attempt flight he would be forced into collision with some of them. Sut was surprised that as yet no indignity had been offered him. As the Apaches had every reason to hate him with the very intensity of hatred, it would have been in keeping with their character to have made his lot as uncomfortable as possible.

"It'll come by-and-bye," he sighed, as the cramped position of his arms pained him. "I don't know what they're waitin' fur. Mebbe they want to get up such a high old time with me that they're writin' out a programme, and have sent to New Orleans fur a band of music. Thar's nothing like doing these things up in style, and I s'pose Lone Wolf means to honor me in that way."

At a late hour, the moon arose, and the light penetrated the ravine, where the strange, motley crowd congregated. The fire still burned, and no one showed any disposition to sleep. By way of relief, the scout lay over upon his side, and was looking up at the clear moon-lit sky when he heard the tramp of horses, and immediately rose up again.

He saw the chieftain, whom he had observed a few hours before, as he came in with his news of the destruction of New Boston, accompanied by two others, all mounted. They rode up in such a position that they surrounded the captive, who was suddenly lifted by a couple of Apaches, and placed astride of the mustang in front of the young chief. The next minute the quartette moved off.

"Skulp me! if I know what this means!" muttered Sut, who felt uneasy over the new turn of affairs. "Things are getting sort of mixed just now."

He hoped that he would learn something of the purpose of the three redskins from their conversation as they rode along; but unfortunately for that hope, they did not exchange a word. When they had ridden a fourth of a mile, Sut caught the flash of a knife in the chieftain's hand. The next instant, it moved swiftly along his back, and the lariat was cut in many pieces. The arms of the scout were freed, although for some minutes they were so benumbed that he could scarcely move them.

What did all this mean? Fully another quarter of a mile was ridden in silence, when the three halted, and Sut felt that the critical moment had arrived. The chief dismounted from the horse, leaving the scout seated thereon. One of the others reached over and handed him his own gun, while the third passed him back his long knife.

"Wall, if I'm to fight all three of yer, sail in!" called out Sut, gathering himself for a charge from them.

They made no reply. The chief vaulted upon one of the other horses, behind the warrior, and, as he did so, a fourth figure advanced and leaped upon the other, so that there were two Indians upon each mustang. The scout scrutinized the new comer, as well as he could in the moonlight.

Yes, there was no mistake about his identity. It was Lone Wolf, who remained as silent as the others.

The heads of the mustangs were turned down the ravine again, and they struck into a gallop, the sound of their hoofs coming back fainter and more faintly, until they died in the night. Sut Simpson was free, and free without a fight, as he realized, when he gave his horse the word, and he dropped into an easy gait in a direction opposite to that taken by the Apaches.

CHAPTER XXVII

THE END

"Wall, that ere little matter was settled without any hard words," muttered the scout, as he rode up the ravine. "It ain't the way Lone Wolf generally manages them things, but that affair me and him had, when I took my hoss away from him, I s'pose had something to do with it."

The scout had considerable cause to feel grateful and pleased over the turn of events. He had his horse and gun, and it now only remained for him to rejoin his companions. He had already passed the point where Mickey O'Rooney had left the ravine, and he felt the impropriety of turning back and presuming upon any further indulgence of the Apaches.

Accordingly, he slackened the speed of his mustang until he reached an avenue of escape. He was forced to go quite a distance before finding one, but he did, at last, and turned his horse into it.

"I don't know whether that ar Irishman can find the way back to whar we left the younker, but I suppose he'll try, so I'll aim at the same p'int."

The night was pretty well gone, and his mustang had

struggled nobly until he showed signs of weariness, and the scout concluded to wait until daylight before pushing his hunt any further. They were miles away from the Apache camp, and he had no fears of disturbance from that quarter. So he drew rein in a secluded spot, and sprang to the ground.

At the very moment of doing so, his horse gave a whinny, which was instantly responded to by a whinny from another horse, less than a hundred feet away.

"That's qua'ar," muttered the scout, as he grasped his rifle. "Whar thar's a hoss in these parts, thar's generally a man, and whar thar's a man, you kin set him down as an Injun. And as this can't be Lone Wolf, I'll find out who he is."

His own mustang being a strayer, he managed to tie him to a small, scrubby bush, after which he moved forward, with caution and stealth, in the direction whence came the whinny that had arrested his attention. His purpose was to prevent the other animal discovering his approach—an exceedingly difficult task, as the mustangs of the Southwest are among the very best sentinels that are known, frequently detecting the approach of danger when their masters fail to do so. However, Sut succeeded in getting so close, that he could plainly detect the outlines of the animal, which was standing motionless, with head erect, and his nose turned in the direction of the other mustang, as though he were all attention, and on the look-out for danger.

The scout paused to study the matter, for he did not understand the precise situation of things. The mustang which he saw might be only one of a dozen others, whose owners were near at hand, with possible several searching for him. The conclusion was inevitable that it was necessary for him to reconnoitre a little further before allowing his own position to be uncovered.

Before he could advance any further, he caught sight of a man, who moved silently forward between him and the horse, where he could be seen with greater distinctness. He held his rifle in hand, and seemed disturbed at the action of his horse, which was clearly an admonition for him to be on his guard.

The scout studied him for a minute, and then cautiously raised the hammer of his rifle. Guarded as was the movement, the faint click caught the ear of the other, who started, and was on the point of leaping back, when Sut called out:

"Stop, or I'll bore a hole through yer!"

The figure did not move.

"Come forward and surrender."

The form remained like a statue.

"Throw down that gun or I'll shoot."

This brought a response, which came in the shape of a well-known voice:

"Not while I have the spirit of a man left, as me uncle observed when his wife commanded him to come down from a tree that she might pummel him. How are ye, old boy?"

The scout had suspected the identity of his friend from the first, and had made the attempt to frighten him from the innate love of the thing. The two grasped hands cordially and were rejoiced beyond measure at this fortunate meeting.

Mickey explained that he had not been scratched by a bullet, nor had his horse suffered injury. It was a most singular escape indeed. But no more singular than that of the scout himself, who had received mercy at the hands of Lone Wolf, who had never been known to be guilty of such a weakness. It had been a providential deliverance all around, and the men could not be otherwise than in the best sprits.

"The next thing is to hunt up the younker," said the scout, as they sat upon the the ground discussing incidents of the past few days. "I'm a little troubled about him, 'cause we've been away longer than we expected, and some of the varmints may have got on his trail."

"How far from this place do ye reckon him to be?"

"That's powerful hard to tell, but it can't be much less than a mile, and that's a good ways in such a hilly country as this. Yer can't git over it faster than yer kin run."

"But ye know the way thar, as I understand ye to remark?"

The scout signified that he would have no more trouble in reaching it then in making his way across a room. They decided, though, that the best thing they could do was to wait where they were until daylight, and then take up the hunt. They remained talking and smoking for an hour or two longer, neither closing their eyes in slumber, although the occasion was improved to its utmost by their animals. The scout was capable of losing a couple of nights' rest without being materially effected thereby, while Mickey's experience almost enabled him to do the same.

As soon as it was fairly light the two were on the move, Sut leading the course in the direction of the spot where they had left Fred Munson the day before, and which he had vacated very suddenly. They were picking their way along as best they could, when they struck a small stream, when the scout paused so suddenly that his comrade inquired the cause.

"That's quar, powerful quar," he said looking down at the ground and speaking as if to himself.

"One horse has been 'long har, and I think it war mine, and that he had that younker on his back."

"Which way was the young spalpeen traveling?"

The scout indicated the course, and then added, in an excited undertone:

"It looks to me as if he got scared out and had to leave, and it ain't no ways likely that anything would have scared him short of Injuns—so it's time we j'ined him."

The Irishman was decidedly of the same opinion, and the trail was at once taken.

"Be the powers! do you mind that?" demanded Mickey, in an excited voice.

"Mind what?" asked the scout, somewhat startled at his manner.

"Jes' look yonder, will ye?"

As he spoke, he pointed up the slope ahead of them. There, but a comparatively short distance away, was Fred Munson, in plain sight, seated upon the back of his mustang, apparently scrutinizing the two horsemen, as if in doubt as to their identity. The parties recognized each other at the same moment, and Fred waved his hat, which salutation was returned by his friends. The scout motioned to him to ride down to where he and Mickey were waiting.

"He's off the trail altogether, and if he keeps on that course, he'll fetch up in New Orleans, or Galveston," he added, by way of explanation.

The lad lost no time in rejoining them, and the trio formed a joyous party. Not one was injured, each had a good swift horse, and a weapon of some kind, and was far better equipped for a homeward journey than they had dared to hope.

"Thar's only one thing to make a slight delay," said the Irishman, after pretty much everything had been explained.

His friends looked to him for an explanation.

"I resaved notice from me family physician in London this mornin', that it was dangerous when in this part of the world to travel on an empty stomach."

All three felt the need of food and Sut considered the spot where they were as good for camping purposes as any they were likely to find. So they dismounted, and while Mickey and Fred busied themselves in gathering wood, and preparing the fire, the scout went off in search of game.

"Do ye mind," called out Mickey, "that ye mustn't return till ye bring something wid ye? I'm so hungry that I'm not particular. A biled Apache will answer, if ye can't find anything else."

"If he gets anything," said Fred, "we must make away with all we can, and try to eat enough to last us two or three days."

"That's what I always do at each meal," promptly replied his friend. "Thar's nothing like being prepared for emergencies, as me cousin, Butt O'Norghoghon, remarked when he presented the gal he was coortin' with a set of teeth and a whig, which she didn't naad any more than does me hoss out thar."

The scout returned before he was expected, and with a superabundance of food, which was cooked and fully enjoyed, and as speedily as possible they were mounted and on the road again. The traveling was exceedingly difficult, and although they struck the main pass near noon, and put their horses to their best speed, yet it was dark when they succeeded in clearing themselves of the mountains and reached the edge of the prairies, which stretched away almost unbrokenly for hundreds of miles. They saw Indians several times but did not exchange shots during the day. It was not a general rule with Sut Simpson to avoid an encounter with redskins, but he did it on the present occasion on account of his companions, and especially for the lad's sake. A safe place for the encampment was selected, the mustangs so placed that they would be certain to detect the approach of any enemies during the night, and all laid down to slumber.

Providence, that had so kindly watched over them through all their perils, did not forget them when they lay stretched helpless upon the ground.

The night passed away without molestation, and, making a breakfast from the cooked meat that they had preserved, they struck out upon the prairie in the direction of New Boston.

They had scarcely started, when a party of Indians, probably Comanches, saw them and gave chase. The pursuers were well mounted, and, for a time, the danger was critical, as they numbered fully twenty; but the mustangs of the fugitives were also fleet of foot, and, at last, they carried them beyond all danger from that source.

As the friends galloped along at an easy pace, Sut Simpson struck them with horror by telling them the story of the massacre, which he had heard discussed among the Apaches when he was a prisoner. All were anxious to learn the extent of the horrible tale, and they pressed their steeds to the utmost.

The site of the town was reached late in the afternoon, when it was speedily seen that the young chief had told the truth. New Boston was among the things of the past, having actually died while in the struggles of birth. The unfinished houses had been burned to the ground, the stock run off, and most of the inhabitants massacred. The fight had been a desperate one, but when Lone Wolf sent his warriors a second time they were resistless, and carried everything before them.

"If any of 'em got away, they've reached Fort Severn," said the scout, who was impressed by the evidences of the terrible scenes that had been enacted here, within a comparatively few hours; "but I don't think thar's much chance."

The remains of those who had fallen on the spot were so mutilated, and in many cases partly burned, that they could not be recognized. Among the wreck and ruin of matter were discovered a number of shovels. The three set themselves to dig a trench, into which all these remains were placed and carefully covered over with earth.

"We'll take a shovel along," said Sut, as he threw one over his shoulder, and sprang upon his horse. "We'll be likely to find need for it afore we reach the fort."

This prediction was verified. As they rode along they

constantly came upon bodies of men and women, whose horses had given out, or who had been shot while fleeing for life. In every case the poor fugitives had been scalped and mutilated. They were gathered up and tenderly buried, with no headstone to mark their remains, there to sleep until the last trump shall sound.

Fort Severn was reached in the afternoon of the second day. There were found, just six men and two women, the fleetness of whose steeds had enabled them to win in the race for life. All the others had fallen, among them Caleb Barnwell, the leader of the Quixotic scheme, and the founder of the town which died with him. The valley of the Rio Pecos was not prepared for any settlement unless one organized upon a scale calculated to overawe all combinations of the Apaches, Commanches, and Kiowas.

From Fort Severn, Mickey O'Rooney and Fred Munson, under the escort, or rather guidance, of Sut Simpson, made their way overland to Fort Aubray, where Mr. Munson, the father of Fred, was found. The latter thanked heaven for the sickness which had detained him and could not fully express his gratitude for the wonderful preservation of Mickey and his son. Sut Simpson, the scout, was well paid for his services, and, bidding them good-bye, he went to his field of duty in the southwest, while Mr. Munson, Mickey and Fred were glad enough to return east.

　　　　Lieut. R. H. Jayne

Choose from Thousands of 1stWorldLibrary Classics By

A. M. Barnard
Ada Leverson
Adolphus William Ward
Aesop
Agatha Christie
Alexander Aaronsohn
Alexander Kielland
Alexandre Dumas
Alfred Gatty
Alfred Ollivant
Alice Duer Miller
Alice Turner Curtis
Alice Dunbar
Allen Chapman
Alleyne Ireland
Ambrose Bierce
Amelia E. Barr
Amory H. Bradford
Andrew Lang
Andrew McFarland Davis
Andy Adams
Angela Brazil
Anna Alice Chapin
Anna Sewell
Annie Besant
Annie Hamilton Donnell
Annie Payson Call
Annie Roe Carr
Annonaymous
Anton Chekhov
Archibald Lee Fletcher
Arnold Bennett
Arthur C. Benson
Arthur Conan Doyle
Arthur M. Winfield
Arthur Ransome
Arthur Schnitzler
Arthur Train
Atticus
B.H. Baden-Powell
B. M. Bower
B. C. Chatterjee
Baroness Emmuska Orczy
Baroness Orczy
Basil King
Bayard Taylor
Ben Macomber
Bertha Muzzy Bower
Bjornstjerne Bjornson

Booth Tarkington
Boyd Cable
Bram Stoker
C. Collodi
C. E. Orr
C. M. Ingleby
Carolyn Wells
Catherine Parr Traill
Charles A. Eastman
Charles Amory Beach
Charles Dickens
Charles Dudley Warner
Charles Farrar Browne
Charles Ives
Charles Kingsley
Charles Klein
Charles Hanson Towne
Charles Lathrop Pack
Charles Romyn Dake
Charles Whibley
Charles Willing Beale
Charlotte M. Braeme
Charlotte M. Yonge
Charlotte Perkins Stetson
Clair W. Hayes
Clarence Day Jr.
Clarence E. Mulford
Clemence Housman
Confucius
Coningsby Dawson
Cornelis DeWitt Wilcox
Cyril Burleigh
D. H. Lawrence
Daniel Defoe
David Garnett
Dinah Craik
Don Carlos Janes
Donald Keyhoe
Dorothy Kilner
Dougan Clark
Douglas Fairbanks
E. Nesbit
E. P. Roe
E. Phillips Oppenheim
E. S. Brooks
Earl Barnes
Edgar Rice Burroughs
Edith Van Dyne
Edith Wharton

Edward Everett Hale
Edward J. O'Biren
Edward S. Ellis
Edwin L. Arnold
Eleanor Atkins
Eleanor Hallowell Abbott
Eliot Gregory
Elizabeth Gaskell
Elizabeth McCracken
Elizabeth Von Arnim
Ellem Key
Emerson Hough
Emilie F. Carlen
Emily Bronte
Emily Dickinson
Enid Bagnold
Enilor Macartney Lane
Erasmus W. Jones
Ernie Howard Pie
Ethel May Dell
Ethel Turner
Ethel Watts Mumford
Eugene Sue
Eugenie Foa
Eugene Wood
Eustace Hale Ball
Evelyn Everett-green
Everard Cotes
F. H. Cheley
F. J. Cross
F. Marion Crawford
Fannie E. Newberry
Federick Austin Ogg
Ferdinand Ossendowski
Fergus Hume
Florence A. Kilpatrick
Fremont B. Deering
Francis Bacon
Francis Darwin
Frances Hodgson Burnett
Frances Parkinson Keyes
Frank Gee Patchin
Frank Harris
Frank Jewett Mather
Frank L. Packard
Frank V. Webster
Frederic Stewart Isham
Frederick Trevor Hill
Frederick Winslow Taylor

Friedrich Kerst
Friedrich Nietzsche
Fyodor Dostoyevsky
G.A. Henty
G.K. Chesterton
Gabrielle E. Jackson
Garrett P. Serviss
Gaston Leroux
George A. Warren
George Ade
Geroge Bernard Shaw
George Cary Eggleston
George Durston
George Ebers
George Eliot
George Gissing
George MacDonald
George Meredith
George Orwell
George Sylvester Viereck
George Tucker
George W. Cable
George Wharton James
Gertrude Atherton
Gordon Casserly
Grace E. King
Grace Gallatin
Grace Greenwood
Grant Allen
Guillermo A. Sherwell
Gulielma Zollinger
Gustav Flaubert
H. A. Cody
H. B. Irving
H.C. Bailey
H. G. Wells
H. H. Munro
H. Irving Hancock
H. R. Naylor
H. Rider Haggard
H. W. C. Davis
Haldeman Julius
Hall Caine
Hamilton Wright Mabie
Hans Christian Andersen
Harold Avery
Harold McGrath
Harriet Beecher Stowe
Harry Castlemon
Harry Coghill
Harry Houidini

Hayden Carruth
Helent Hunt Jackson
Helen Nicolay
Hendrik Conscience
Hendy David Thoreau
Henri Barbusse
Henrik Ibsen
Henry Adams
Henry Ford
Henry Frost
Henry James
Henry Jones Ford
Henry Seton Merriman
Henry W Longfellow
Herbert A. Giles
Herbert Carter
Herbert N. Casson
Herman Hesse
Hildegard G. Frey
Homer
Honore De Balzac
Horace B. Day
Horace Walpole
Horatio Alger Jr.
Howard Pyle
Howard R. Garis
Hugh Lofting
Hugh Walpole
Humphry Ward
Ian Maclaren
Inez Haynes Gillmore
Irving Bacheller
Isabel Cecilia Williams
Isabel Hornibrook
Israel Abrahams
Ivan Turgenev
J.G.Austin
J. Henri Fabre
J. M. Barrie
J. M. Walsh
J. Macdonald Oxley
J. R. Miller
J. S. Fletcher
J. S. Knowles
J. Storer Clouston
J. W. Duffield
Jack London
Jacob Abbott
James Allen
James Andrews
James Baldwin

James Branch Cabell
James DeMille
James Joyce
James Lane Allen
James Lane Allen
James Oliver Curwood
James Oppenheim
James Otis
James R. Driscoll
Jane Abbott
Jane Austen
Jane L. Stewart
Janet Aldridge
Jens Peter Jacobsen
Jerome K. Jerome
Jessie Graham Flower
John Buchan
John Burroughs
John Cournos
John F. Kennedy
John Gay
John Glasworthy
John Habberton
John Joy Bell
John Kendrick Bangs
John Milton
John Philip Sousa
John Taintor Foote
Jonas Lauritz Idemil Lie
Jonathan Swift
Joseph A. Altsheler
Joseph Carey
Joseph Conrad
Joseph E. Badger Jr
Joseph Hergesheimer
Joseph Jacobs
Jules Vernes
Julian Hawthrone
Julie A Lippmann
Justin Huntly McCarthy
Kakuzo Okakura
Karle Wilson Baker
Kate Chopin
Kenneth Grahame
Kenneth McGaffey
Kate Langley Bosher
Kate Langley Bosher
Katherine Cecil Thurston
Katherine Stokes
L. A. Abbot
L. T. Meade

L. Frank Baum
Latta Griswold
Laura Dent Crane
Laura Lee Hope
Laurence Housman
Lawrence Beasley
Leo Tolstoy
Leonid Andreyev
Lewis Carroll
Lewis Sperry Chafer
Lilian Bell
Lloyd Osbourne
Louis Hughes
Louis Joseph Vance
Louis Tracy
Louisa May Alcott
Lucy Fitch Perkins
Lucy Maud Montgomery
Luther Benson
Lydia Miller Middleton
Lyndon Orr
M. Corvus
M. H. Adams
Margaret E. Sangster
Margret Howth
Margaret Vandercook
Margaret W. Hungerford
Margret Penrose
Maria Edgeworth
Maria Thompson Daviess
Mariano Azuela
Marion Polk Angellotti
Mark Overton
Mark Twain
Mary Austin
Mary Catherine Crowley
Mary Cole
Mary Hastings Bradley
Mary Roberts Rinehart
Mary Rowlandson
M. Wollstonecraft Shelley
Maud Lindsay
Max Beerbohm
Myra Kelly
Nathaniel Hawthrone
Nicolo Machiavelli
O. F. Walton
Oscar Wilde

Owen Johnson
P.G. Wodehouse
Paul and Mabel Thorne
Paul G. Tomlinson
Paul Severing
Percy Brebner
Percy Keese Fitzhugh
Peter B. Kyne
Plato
Quincy Allen
R. Derby Holmes
R. L. Stevenson
R. S. Ball
Rabindranath Tagore
Rahul Alvares
Ralph Bonehill
Ralph Henry Barbour
Ralph Victor
Ralph Waldo Emmerson
Rene Descartes
Ray Cummings
Rex Beach
Rex E. Beach
Richard Harding Davis
Richard Jefferies
Richard Le Gallienne
Robert Barr
Robert Frost
Robert Gordon Anderson
Robert L. Drake
Robert Lansing
Robert Lynd
Robert Michael Ballantyne
Robert W. Chambers
Rosa Nouchette Carey
Rudyard Kipling
Saint Augustine
Samuel B. Allison
Samuel Hopkins Adams
Sarah Bernhardt
Sarah C. Hallowell
Selma Lagerlof
Sherwood Anderson
Sigmund Freud
Standish O'Grady
Stanley Weyman
Stella Benson
Stella M. Francis

Stephen Crane
Stewart Edward White
Stijn Streuvels
Swami Abhedananda
Swami Parmananda
T. S. Ackland
T. S. Arthur
The Princess Der Ling
Thomas A. Janvier
Thomas A Kempis
Thomas Anderton
Thomas Bailey Aldrich
Thomas Bulfinch
Thomas De Quincey
Thomas Dixon
Thomas H. Huxley
Thomas Hardy
Thomas More
Thornton W. Burgess
U. S. Grant
Upton Sinclair
Valentine Williams
Various Authors
Vaughan Kester
Victor Appleton
Victor G. Durham
Victoria Cross
Virginia Woolf
Wadsworth Camp
Walter Camp
Walter Scott
Washington Irving
Wilbur Lawton
Wilkie Collins
Willa Cather
Willard F. Baker
William Dean Howells
William le Queux
W. Makepeace Thackeray
William W. Walter
William Shakespeare
Winston Churchill
Yei Theodora Ozaki
Yogi Ramacharaka
Young E. Allison
Zane Grey